PLAYFUL

FUN PROJECTS TO MAKE WITH + FOR KIDS

MERRILEE LIDDIARD

PHOTOGRAPHS BY NICOLE HILL GERULAT

STC CRAFT | A MELANIE FALICK BOOK | NEW YORK

Published in 2014 by Stewart, Tabori & Chang
An imprint of ABRAMS.

Text and illustrations copyright © 2014 Merrilee Liddiard
Photographs copyright © 2014 Nicole Hill Gerulat

Library of Congress Control Number: 2014930835
ISBN: 978-1-61769-045-7

Editor: Melanie Falick
Designer: Brooke Reynolds for inchmark
Production Manager: Tina Cameron
Photographer: Nicole Hill Gerulat
Photo Assistant: Cassidy Tuttle
Set & Props: Meta Coleman
Wardrobe: Brittany Watson Jepsen
Hair & Makeup: Aubrey Nelson & Kamra Christensen

The text of this book was composed in Avenir.

Printed and bound in China.

10 9 8 7 6 5 4 3 2 1

Stewart, Tabori & Chang books are available at special discounts when purchased in quantity for premiums and promotions as well as fundraising or educational use. Special editions can also be created to specification. For details, contact specialsales@abramsbooks.com or the address below.

THE ART OF BOOKS SINCE 1949

115 West 18th Street
New York, NY 10011
www.abramsbooks.com

TO MY LITTLE ONES

CONTENTS

GETTING SET FOR THE ART OF PLAY

I grew up in a home that was constantly filled with the busy hum of creativity, handmade magic, and playfulness.

Throughout the year, my father could be found crafting dollhouses from cardboard or creating giant wooden jigsaw puzzles. I would often hear the buzz of my mother's sewing machine while she toiled away making dolls, dress-up clothes, and dreams come true. It didn't take long for me, or my eight siblings, to pick up the fervor of creation and join in on all the playful fun!

I can vividly remember at a young age poring over and pawing through vintage books, discarded tin cans, bottle tops, refrigerator boxes, and more, looking for ways to make these things new with my hands. And then at the age of twelve, I started my own tradition of taking paper plates, construction paper, and glue to my babysitting appointments. Together, the kids and I would cut and paste until we created our very own zoo of paper-plate masks (see page 119 for my latest iteration of this project). It was great fun! Creation and imagination were such a vivid and important part of my growing years.

Later, I took this love for creation and art even further and went to art school to study illustration. I got married, moved to New York, and began illustrating professionally, creating the art for children's books, television commercials, toys, games, and more.

When my husband and I had our first child, like all parents, I loved to watch my son grow and observe the sorts of things he gravitated toward and responded to. Patterns, puzzles, repetition, shapes, and bold, simple colors were among the many things he loved. I then had my second son,

who was a huge fan of moving parts, characters, and imaginative play. Their inclinations spoke to me, and I very quickly began making them toys, drawing for them, and creating activities to encourage further playful exploration that met their learning styles. I also began to blog about our creative adventures on mermagblog.com, encouraging other parents to share in our love of play with their own families. Puppets, puzzles, and more were born. And just as I did as a child, I often found myself scouring the pantry for discarded boxes, bottle tops, and other objects to help create these playful toys. As a result, I have seen firsthand how important the influence of creative play is on young people and how it encourages their ability to problem-solve, boosts their confidence, releases tension, and so much more. We now have a baby girl who is opening up an entirely new world of play to us. In short, we have very decidedly made our home a creative and playful one.

Introducing and encouraging creation and the art of play in your home is not only enriching and educational, but can also be quite easy and fun! Don't be afraid to incorporate moments of playfulness in and around your home. Sneak a costume box in your living room so that your little ones can become noble knights and fair maidens (pages 28–57), embarking on quests and casting magical spells at a moment's notice. Or go on a nature walk and collect twigs, then make a magical crown (page 59) from your forest findings.

Create simple yet beautiful toys, such as a Squiggle Floor Tile Puzzle (page 75) that are not

Left to right: Duct Tape
Cardboard Brownstone
(page 107), Duct Tape
Bird Costume (page 121),
Paper Plate Animal Mask
(page 19).

only educational but are so pretty you won't mind them being strewn across the floor!

Simple, colorful paper in all shapes, patterns, and textures is a great way to start young imaginations flowing. Set up a creative workstation and keep stacks of it on hand to inspire paper-puppet parades (page 13) and delicate floral crowns (page 23).

Designate a box, drawer, or shelf and fill it with recycled treasures and household items such as discarded cracker boxes, paper plates, and duct tape. Let your little ones scrounge through and create repurposed treasures (page 111).

And keep playful art supplies on hand in a fun way, such as stashing them in funny face pencil holders (page 103), to inspire your little one to make masterpieces.

When you set the stage for the art of play in your home and learning environment, you are opening up a very special world for your little ones. And let's not forget—it's so much fun for you, too! The projects in this book are designed to encourage this playfulness and creativity. Some can be done by children alone and some require adult supervision.

So what are we waiting for? Let's get started!

PLAYFUL PAPER CRAFTS

PAPER PUPPET PARADE

Your little one and their pals will be parading around their handmade paper zoo with these fun and easy puppets.

MATERIALS

1 sheet each standard-size poster board (22-by-28-inch/ 56-by-71-cm) in red, black, orange, and navy blue for horse, bear, fox, and bird

2 sheets standard-size poster board in light blue for elephant

Extra poster board or cardstock in blue, pink, yellow, and white for features such as cheeks, beak, and bear nose

Scissors

Pencil

Tape or glue

Hole punch or other sharp, pointed object

Large brads

½-by-36-inch (1.3-by-91 cm) dowels (optional)

Duct tape, optional

HORSE

1 Photocopy or scan and print the horse template (see pullout sheet inside back cover) at 200%. Cut out the pattern pieces.

2 Trace the head, body, and legs onto red poster board and cut out the shapes.

3 Trace the eye onto blue and cut out.

4 Trace the mane onto light blue and cut out.

5 Trace the tail onto dark blue and cut out.

6 Trace the cheek onto hot pink and cut out.

7 Glue the eye, cheek, and mane onto the horse's head, referring to the project photograph above for placement.

8 Punch or poke small holes into the pieces where indicated on the template. Using brads, attach the head, legs, and tail onto the horse's body.

9 Play with the horse as is, or tape two wooden dowels to the back of the horse body, one toward the front and one toward the back, for a puppet parade!

BEAR

1 Photocopy or scan and print the bear template (see pullout sheet inside back cover) at 200%. Cut out the pattern pieces.

2 Trace the head, body, legs, and tail onto black poster board (use a white colored pencil if you have trouble seeing the traced line). Cut out the shapes.

3 Trace the snout onto yellow poster board or cardstock and cut out.

4 Trace the nose onto red and cut out.

5 Trace the eye onto white and cut out.

6 Trace the cheek onto hot pink and cut out.

7 Glue the snout onto the bear's head and then glue the nose on top of the snout.

8 Glue the eye and cheek onto the head.

9 Punch or poke small holes into the pieces where indicated on the template. Using brads, attach the head, legs, and tail onto the bear's body.

10 Play with the bear as is or tape two wooden dowels onto the back of the bear body, one toward the front and one toward the back, for a puppet parade!

FOX

1 Photocopy or scan and print the fox template (see pullout sheet inside back cover) at 200%. Cut out the pattern pieces.

2 Trace the head, body, legs, and tail onto orange poster board. Cut out.

3 Trace the eye onto light blue poster board or cardstock and cut out.

4 Trace the scarf onto blue and cut out.

5 Trace the nose onto black and cut out.

6 Trace the cheek onto hot pink and cut out.

7 Glue the eye, nose, and cheek onto the fox's head.

8 Punch or poke small holes into the fox pieces where indicated on the template. Using brads, attach the head, scarf, legs, and tail onto the body.

9 Play with the fox as is, or tape two wooden dowels onto the back of the fox body, one toward the front and one toward the back, for a puppet parade!

BIRD

1 Photocopy or scan and print the bird template (see pullout sheet inside back cover) at 200%. Cut out the pattern pieces.

2 Trace the body and wing base onto dark blue poster board and cut out.

3 Trace the beak onto yellow poster board or cardstock and cut out.

4 Trace the tail and main wing piece onto red and cut out.

5 Trace the cheek and second wing scallop onto hot pink and cut out.

6 Trace the eye and third wing scallop onto light blue and cut out.

7 Trace the fourth wing scallop out of orange and cut out.

8 Glue the eye, cheek, and beak onto the bird's face.

9 Glue all the wing scallops onto the wing base.

10 Punch or poke small holes into the bird pieces where indicated on the template. Using brads, attach the wing and tail to the bird's body.

11 Play with the bird as is or tape a wooden dowel onto the back of the bird for a puppet parade!

ELEPHANT

1 Photocopy or scan and print the elephant template (see pullout sheet inside back cover) at 200%. Cut out the pattern pieces.

2 Trace the body and head onto light blue poster board and cut out.

3 Trace the ear onto red cardstock and cut out.

4 Trace the tail onto dark blue cardstock and cut out.

5 Trace the eye onto blue cardstock and cut out.

6 Trace the cheek and toenails onto hot pink cardstock and cut out.

7 Glue the eye and cheek onto the elephant's face.

8 Punch or poke small holes into the elephant pieces where indicated on the template.

9 Using brads, attach the head, ear, and tail to the elephant's body.

10 Play with the elephant as is, or tape two wooden dowels onto the back of the elephant body, one toward the front and one toward the back, for a puppet parade!

TIPS
Print out the animal templates at smaller sizes and use them as shadow puppets or even cupcake toppers.

Of course the sky is the limit when it comes to color choices. Follow my lead, or choose your own!

PAPER PLATE ANIMAL MASKS

Kids will love transforming into playful animals with these fun and easy animal masks made from paper plates!

MATERIALS

Colorful cardstock

Pencil

Scissors

1¼- and 2-inch (3- and 5-cm) hole punches, for eye shapes (optional)

Standard (about 9-inch/23-cm) paper plates

Glue

Straw or pencil to hold mask up; or elastic to hold mask on

Tape

PANDA MASK

1 Photocopy or trace the Panda templates on pages 124 and 125 at 100% and cut out the shapes.

2 Trace the template pieces onto colorful cardstock and cut out the shapes (A). (You can use circle punches for the eye pieces, if you have them.)

3 Hold a paper plate to your face and note where the eyeholes should be. Mark the eye placement on the plate. Cut out the eyeholes, making them just a tad larger than the inside of the eye shapes you cut from cardstock.

4 Glue all the panda features onto the plate (the ears can be attached to the backside of the plate), referring to the project photograph at left and B for placement.

5 When you are happy with your panda face, attach a straw or pencil to the back of the plate with strong tape and use it to hold up the mask (C). Or punch a hole on either side of the plate and tie on a strip of elastic for your little jungle animal to roam around hands-free!

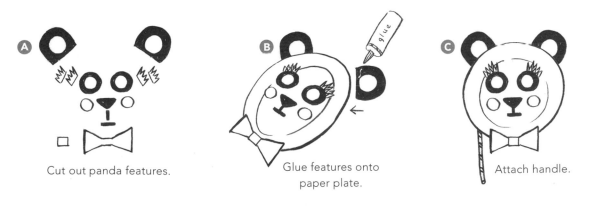

Cut out panda features.

Glue features onto paper plate.

Attach handle.

Cut out lion features.

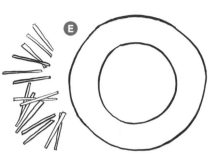

Cut out lion's mane and contrasting paper strips.

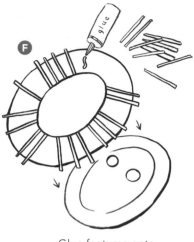

Glue features onto paper plate.

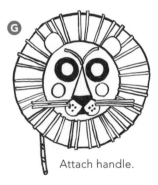

Attach handle.

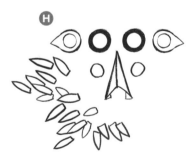

Cut out bird features.

Glue features onto paper plate.

Attach handle.

LION MASK

1 Photocopy or trace the lion templates on page 125 at 100% and cut out the shapes.

2 Trace the template pieces onto colorful cardstock and cut out the shapes (**D**). (You can use circle punches for the eye pieces, if you have them.)

3 Hold a paper plate to your face and note where the eyeholes should be. Mark the eye placement on the plate. Cut out the eyeholes, making them just a tad larger than the inside of the eye shapes you cut from cardstock.

4 Make the lion's mane by tracing the outer edge of your paper plate onto a piece of cardstock. Trace the inner edge of the plate inside the first circle you created, and cut out the ring to create the mane base (**E**). Cut several thin strips of a contrasting-color cardstock (**E**) and glue them onto the base (**F**).

5 Glue all the other features onto the paper plate, referring to the project photograph and **G** for placement.

6 When you are happy with your lion face, attach a straw or pencil to the back of the plate with strong tape and use it to hold up the mask (**G**). Or punch a hole on either side of the plate and tie on a strip of elastic for your little jungle animal to roam around hands-free!

BIRD MASK

1 Photocopy or trace the bird templates on page 124 at 100% and cut out the shapes.

2 Trace the template pieces onto colorful cardstock and cut out the shapes. (You can use circle punches for the eye pieces, if you have them.) Cut out several curved triangular shapes from colorful cardstock for the bird's feathers (**H**).

3 Hold a paper plate to your face and note where the eyeholes should be. Mark the eye placement on the plate. Cut out the eyeholes, making them just a tad larger than the inside of the eye shapes you cut from cardstock.

4 Fold the bird beak piece in half lengthwise. Fold the side tabs under and run a strip of glue along each tab on the side that will be adhered to the paper plate.

5 Referring to the project photograph on page 18 for placement and **I**, set the beak on the paper plate with the glue-coated pieces down, pressing on the tabs from the underside of the beak to affix the glue.

6 Glue all the remaining features onto the paper plate, referring to the project photograph for placement.

7 Glue the feathers around the edge of the plate, attaching them to the back side of the plate (**I**).

8 When you are happy with your bird face, attach a straw or pencil to the back of the plate with strong tape and use it to hold up the mask (**J**). Or punch a hole on either side of the plate and tie on a strip of elastic for your little jungle animal to roam around hands-free!

PAPER FLORAL CROWN

Your little wood nymph will enter a world of imagination with this delicate crown.

MATERIALS

1 sheet standard-size (22-by-28-inch/56-by-71-cm) poster board, for crown

Colorful cardstock, for flowers

Scissors

Utility knife

Hole punch

Three colorful brads (alternatively, paint the heads of the brads in the colors of your choice)

Large glue dot

1 Photocopy, cut out, and trace the crown template (see pullout sheet inside back cover) onto the poster board at 100%. Photocopy, cut out, and trace the exterior flowers onto different-colored cardstock at 100%.

2 Carefully cut out the crown shape and exterior flowers using scissors and a utility knife for the intricate details.

3 Punch holes where indicated on the templates for the exterior flowers and crown.

4 Using brads, attach the colorful exterior flowers to the floral crown.

5 Measure the circumference of your child's head and then secure the back of the crown with the glue dot so the crown fits snugly. Cut any excess from the ends of the crown band.

TIGER PIÑATA

Make your next party a roaring success
with this wild piñata!

MATERIALS

Scissors

Utility knife and cutting mat
(optional)

Two 48-by-72-inch (122-by-183-cm)
sheets cardboard

Masking tape

Hot glue gun

Hot glue sticks

Mod Podge

Foam paint brush

White tissue paper

Black, orange, white, and hot pink
cardstock (or colors of your choice)

String

Candy or other treats to fill piñata

1 Using scissors or a utility knife and cutting mat, cut the following shapes from the cardboard **(A)**:

- Two 24-inch (61-cm) circles for the face

- Four ear shapes (photocopy, cut out, and trace the ear templates found on page 126)

- Two long rectangular strips at least 16 inches (41 cm) long by 3½ inches (9 cm) wide for
ear panels

- One large rectangular strip at least 75 inches (190 cm) long and about 6 inches (15 cm) wide;
join pieces with tape to make up the length

- One 2-inch (5-cm) circle for hanging the piñata

2 To make the face box, using masking tape, tape the large rectangular strip around one circle,
keeping the rectangular strip perpendicular to the outside edge of the cardboard circle **(B)**. Tape the
second circle to the opposite edge of the rectangular strip to form a round box.

3 To make the ears, using masking tape, tape one of the rectangular ear panels around one of the
ear shapes, with the ear panel perpendicular to the outside edge of the ear shape. Tape a second ear
shape to the opposite edge of the ear panel. Repeat with the remaining ear shapes and rectangular
panel to form the other ear.

4 Hot-glue the ears to the tiger face box **(C)**.

5 Using Mod Podge and a small brush, decoupage the white tissue paper onto the tiger face box
and ears until the cardboard is completely covered **(D)**. Let dry completely.

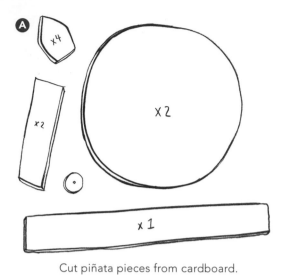

Ⓐ x4 x2 X 2 x 1

Cut piñata pieces from cardboard.

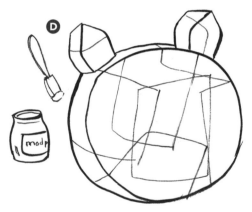

Ⓑ

Tape large rectangular strip around first circle.

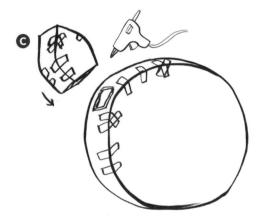

Ⓒ

Hot-glue ears to tiger face box.

Ⓓ mod p

Decoupage tissue paper onto box.

Ⓔ

Finished piñata.

6 Photocopy or scan and print the tiger face templates on page 126 at 200%. Cut out the shapes and trace them onto the appropriate colors of cardstock, according to the project photo below. Cut the tiger face shapes from the cardstock.

7 When the tiger face box and ears are dry, glue the cardstock pieces onto the face and ears, referring to the project photo and **E** for placement. Let dry.

8 Cut a small flap in the bottom of the tiger face box, making sure to leave the flap attached so you can tape it closed later.

9 Using scissors or a utility knife, poke a hole through the center of the 2-inch (5-cm) cardboard circle, and another halfway between the ears on the tiger face box.

10 Knot one end of a long length of string. Run other side of the string through the hole in the small cardboard disc. Pull it down until it rests on the knot.

11 Insert the string/cardboard disc through the hole in the bottom of the piñata and run it through the top hole so that the cardboard disc stops at the top of the piñata interior. Extend the string to the desired length and trim.

12 Fill the piñata with candy or other goodies through the opening at the bottom, and then tape the flap shut. Cover it with more white tissue paper and Mod Podge, if you wish, and let dry.

13 Hang up your new tiger piñata at your next party and swing away!

PLAYFUL DRESS UP

KNIGHT SMOCK

Your young knight easily transforms into one of King Arthur's finest in this simple smock, which is likely to fit an average-size four- to nine-year-old child.

MATERIALS

1 yard (1 m) canvas

Fabric scissors

Straight pins

Tape

Permanent fabric marker

6 yards (5.5 m) extra-wide (½-inch/1.3-cm) double-fold bias tape

Sewing machine

Cotton thread in color to match bias tape

1 Photocopy or scan and print the Knight Smock front, back, and side templates (see pullout sheet inside back cover) at 100%. (Many copy shops provide large-format black-and-white prints at reasonable prices.) Cut out the pattern pieces.

2 Spread the canvas out on a flat surface. Pin the pattern pieces on the fabric, folding the side portion in half to cut two pieces each of back and side **(A)**.

3 Cut out the pieces.

4 Photocopy or scan and print the lion or bear emblem on pages 127 or 128 at 100%.

5 Tape the emblem image facedown on the wrong side of the front, then flip the fabric over. Using a light table or with the image and fabric pressed against a sunny window, trace the drawing onto the fabric using a fabric marker. Remove the template and tape. (Alternatively, skip the emblem templates and draw on your own design freehand.)

6 Encase the lower edge of the front in double-fold bias tape, placing the narrower edge of the bias tape on the right side of the fabric. Using a sewing machine and thread to match the bias tape, stitch the layers of bias tape and fabric together, stitching close to the inner edge of the bias tape **(B)**.

7 Encase the back opening and lower edge of one back piece in double-fold bias tape, placing the narrower edge on the right side of the fabric. Stitch the layers of bias tape and fabric together, stitching close to the inner edge of the bias tape. Repeat with the other back piece. **(C)**

8 Pin the front and back sections together at the shoulders, with right sides facing. The bias-taped edges of the back pieces should be parallel to each other down the middle back of the smock. Using a ¼-inch (6-mm) seam allowance, stitch the front and back together at the shoulders, leaving the sides open. **(D)**

Pin and cut out pattern pieces.

Attach bias tape to lower
edge of smock front.

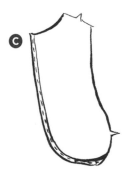

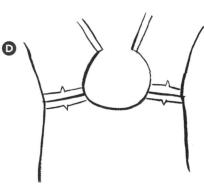

Attach bias tape to back
openings of smock.

Sew front and back
together at shoulders.

Attach bias tape to top and
bottom edges of side pieces.

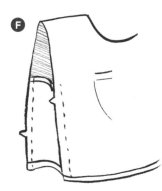

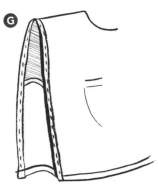

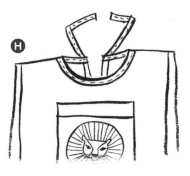

Attach sides to smock.

Attach bias tape to
armhole edges.

Create back tie.

9 Encase the upper and lower edges of one side piece in bias tape and stitch together as before. Repeat with the other side piece (**E**).

10 With wrong sides together, pin one side to the front and back, aligning the bottom edge. Using a ¼-inch (6-mm) seam allowance, stitch the pieces together. Repeat with the other side piece (**F**).

11 Encase the armhole edges for both sides in bias tape, and stitch together as before (**G**).

12 To create a back tie, encase the neck edge in the remaining bias tape, positioning the center of the piece of bias tape at the center front of the neck and extending the ends evenly at center back. You should have two tails of bias tape. Turn the ends of the bias tape in by ¼ inch (6 mm). Stitch as before, close to the inner edge, and then stitch the folded end of each bias tape tail to finish the back tie (**H**).

SWORD AND SHIELD

Your little ones will be fighting dragons in Camelot in no time with these simple cardboard swords and shields that they can make themselves!

MATERIALS

Pencil

1 large sheet of heavy-duty cardboard, approximately 22 by 28 inches (56 by 71 cm)

Utility knife

Cutting mat

Silver duct tape

Hot glue gun

Hot glue sticks

Acrylic or poster paint in the color of your choice

Small dishes or cups, for holding paint

Broad paintbrush

KNIGHT SWORD

1 Freehand or photocopy the sword templates (see pullout sheet inside back cover) at 100%. Cut them out. Trace the templates onto cardboard. With adult help, cut out the pieces with a knife on a cutting mat, making sure the corrugation runs vertically on the sword blade (from top to bottom).

2 Cover the blade portion of the sword with duct tape, leaving the bottom 3 or 4 inches (8 or 10 cm) of cardboard exposed. This will be the sword's handle.

3 With adult help, place a dot of hot glue in the middle of one handle crosspiece. Adhere the crosspiece to the sword handle at the point where the duct tape ends. Flip the sword blade and crosspiece over so the crosspiece is flat on your work surface. Apply hot glue to the side of the crosspiece facing up, as well as to the portion of the sword blade that will be sandwiched between the crosspieces. Place the other crosspiece on top and press it against the glue to adhere. Let the glue dry.

KNIGHT SHIELD

1 Freehand or photocopy the shield and fleur-de-lis templates (see pullout sheet inside back cover) at 100%. Cut them out. Set the fleur-de-lis template piece aside. (Alternatively, skip the fleur-de-lis and paint on a different decoration freehand.)

2 Trace the shield shape onto the remaining cardboard. With adult help, use a utility knife and cutting mat to cut out the shield from the cardboard.

3 To make the handle, roll out 13 inches (33 cm) of duct tape and place the strip on your work surface with the sticky side facing up.

4 Roll out another piece of duct tape the same length and place it onto the first strip of tape, with their sticky sides together.

5 Curve the "ribbon" of duct tape so that it makes a full circle, with overlapping ends. Cut four 4-inch (10-cm) pieces of duct tape and use two of them to secure the duct tape circle vertically to the back of the shield; make sure to place the overlapping ends against the shield. Use the remaining two pieces to reinforce the strips holding the handle to the shield by placing one strip vertically across the ends of both horizontal strips on each side.

6 Turn the shield right side up on your work surface. Trace the fleur-de-lis onto the center front of the shield, if desired.

7 Pour a pool of paint into a small dish or cup. Using a broad paintbrush, paint a strip around the edges of the shield and fill in the fleur-de-lis shape. Let the paint dry. Wash and dry your paintbrush.

8 Now put on your knight smock (page 31) and let the dragon slaying begin!

TIP

Instead of the fleur-de-lis, try other motifs on the shield, such as stripes or a crisscross.

KNIGHT HORSE

Whether galloping off to grand adventures or putting on an equestrian puppet show, your little noble is sure to be enchanted with this versatile play horse puppet.

MATERIALS

All-purpose scissors

Two 20-inch (51-cm) square pieces of canvas

Pencil

Black fabric paint, or color of your choice

Paintbrush

Fabric scissors

Straight pins

Hand-sewing needle or sewing machine

Thread in color of choice

Light piece of fabric such as a kitchen towel

Iron

16-inch (41-cm) piece extra-wide (½-inch/1.3-cm) double-fold bias tape

Broomstick or long, thin tree branch (optional)

1 Photocopy or scan and print the horse head template (see pullout sheet inside back cover) at 100%. Cut out the template piece.

2 With pencil, lightly trace Outline A and Outline B from the template onto the middle of one canvas square. Pencil in the mane and other details from the template (A). Repeat on the second canvas square, flipping the template to create a mirror image of the horse head.

3 Paint over the pencil outline of the horse's head (Outline B) and the penciled details with black fabric paint (B). Repeat on the other sheet of canvas. Let both pieces dry completely.

Trace horse outline onto both canvas squares.

Paint over outline.

4 Using fabric scissors, trim both canvas pieces to the unpainted penciled Outline A **(C)**.

5 With right sides together, pin the canvas pieces together around the edges, leaving the bottom open.

6 Using a ¼-inch (6-mm) seam allowance, sew around the outside of the horse head, being sure to leave the bottom open **(D)**. Trim the outside seam.

7 Turn the horse head right side out through the open bottom **(E)**.

8 Place a piece of light fabric over the horse head sleeve to protect it and press with an iron.

9 Pin the bias tape around the raw open bottom edge **(F)**. Sew the bias tape to the horse head sleeve to finish the edge.

10 You now have a completed play horse sleeve. Place it over a stick for galloping fun or simply use it as a hand puppet.

Trim canvas around artwork.

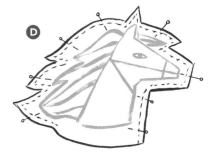

Pin and sew front and back together.

Turn right side out.

Attach bias tape to bottom edge.

FAIR MAIDEN SMOCK

Enter a world of fantasy and make-believe with this simple smock, which is likely to fit an average-size four- to nine-year-old child.

MATERIALS

2 yards (1.8 m) canvas

Fabric scissors

Straight pins

Tape

Permanent fabric marker

12 yards (11 m) extra-wide (½-inch/1.3-cm) double-fold bias tape

Sewing machine

Cotton thread in color to match bias tape

1 Photocopy or scan and print the Fair Maiden Smock front, back, and side templates (see pullout sheet inside back cover) at 100%. (Many copy shops provide large-format black-and-white prints at reasonable prices.) Cut out the pattern pieces.

2 Spread the canvas out on a flat surface. Pin the pattern pieces on the fabric, folding the side portion in half to cut two pieces each of the back and side templates (**A**).

3 Cut out the pieces.

4 Photocopy or scan and print the unicorn emblem on page 129 at 100%.

5 Tape the unicorn image facedown on the wrong side of the front, then flip the fabric over. Using a light table or with the image and fabric pressed against a sunny window, trace the unicorn drawing onto the fabric using a fabric marker. Remove the template and tape. (Alternatively, omit the emblem template and draw your own image freehand.)

6 Encase the lower edge of the front in double-fold bias tape, placing the narrower edge of the tape on the right side of the fabric. Using a sewing machine and thread to match the bias tape, stitch the layers of tape and fabric together, keeping close to the inner edge of the bias tape (**B**).

7 Encase the back opening and lower edge of one back piece in bias tape, placing the narrower edge on the right side of the fabric. Stitch the layers of tape and fabric together, keeping close to the inner edge of the bias tape (**C**). Repeat with the other back piece.

8 Pin the front and back sections together at the shoulders, with right sides facing. The bias-taped edges of the back pieces should be parallel to each other down the middle back of the smock. Using a ¼-inch (6-mm) seam allowance, stitch the front and back together at the shoulders, leaving the sides open (**D**).

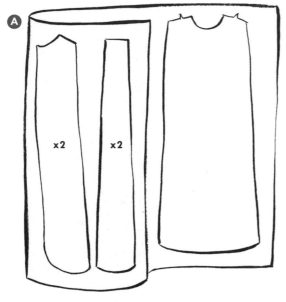

Pin and cut out pattern pieces.

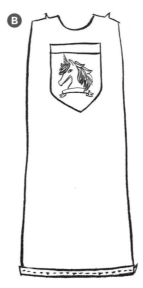

Attach bias tape to lower edge of smock front.

Attach bias tape to back openings of smock.

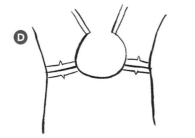

Sew front and back together at shoulders.

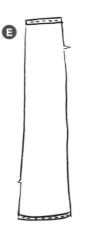

Attach bias tape to top and bottom edges of side pieces.

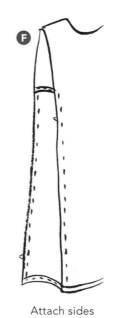

Attach sides to smock.

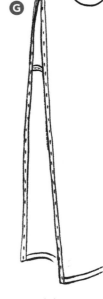

Attach bias tape to armhole edges.

Create back tie.

9 Encase the upper and lower edges of one side piece in bias tape and stitch together as before (**E**). Repeat with the other side.

10 With wrong sides together, pin one side to the front and back, aligning the bottom edges. Using a ¼-inch (6-mm) seam allowance, stitch the pieces together (**F**). Repeat with the second side.

11 Encase the armhole edges in bias tape, and stitch together as before (**G**).

12 To create a back tie, encase the neck edge in the remaining bias tape, positioning the center of the piece of bias tape at the center front of the neck and extending the ends evenly at center back. You should have two tails of bias tape. Turn the ends of the tape in by ¼ inch (6 mm). Stitch as before, close to the inner edge, and then stitch the folded end of each bias tape tail to finish the back tie (**H**).

FAIR MAIDEN CROWN

Your little princess will love getting her hands dirty while making this fun and simple papier-mâché crown.

MATERIALS

Saucepan

Whisk

All-purpose flour

Scissors

Pencil

Poster board

Glue dots or double-sided tape

Newsprint

Waxed paper

Foam brush

Acrylic craft paint in a color of your choice

Contrasting paint color

Round hole punch

Craft glue

Glitter

Two 18-inch (46-cm) ribbons

1 In a saucepan, combine ½ cup (120 ml) flour with 2 cups (475 ml) water (you may need to make a second batch of paste later on). Bring the mixture to a boil, whisking occasionally to dissolve any clumps of flour, then remove from the heat and set aside to cool. Allow to cool completely before using.

2 Photocopy or scan and print the crown template (see pullout sheet inside back cover) at 100% and cut it out. Trace the crown shape onto the poster board and cut it out with scissors.

3 Bring the edges of the crown together to meet at the dashed line. Secure them with glue dots or double-sided tape **(A)**.

4 Cut the newsprint into about 2 inch (5 cm) wide strips. One at a time, dip the newsprint strips into the paste. Use your fingers to brush off excess paste, then apply the strips to the crown, wrapping them around the crown from the base up **(B)**. Continue applying newsprint to the crown until it is completely covered, then repeat up to three times.

5 Set the crown aside on a piece of waxed paper to dry. Once the crown is completely dry, paint the entire crown in the color of your choice. Let it dry. Using a contrasting paint color, paint 2½-inch (6-cm) scallops on the bottom edge **(C)**. Let dry.

6 When the paint is dry, punch a hole on each side of the bottom edge of the crown. Brush a thin layer of glue all around the bottom inch (2.5 cm) of the crown **(D)**. Shake glitter over the glue, covering it entirely **(E)**. Set the crown aside to let the glue dry.

7 Tie a knot at one end of each ribbon and thread one ribbon through each hole in the crown, with the knot on the inside.

8 Secure the crown to your child's head by tying the ribbons in a bow.

9 Enjoy playing dress up for the rest of the afternoon!

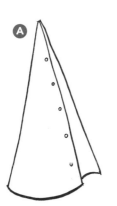

A

Secure edges of crown with glue dots or tape.

B

Apply newsprint strips.

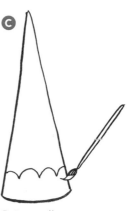

C

Paint scallops.

D

Brush on glue along bottom edge.

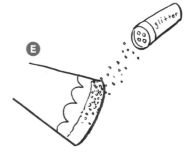

E

Cover glue with glitter.

TIPS
Use a strand of elastic instead of ribbon to hold the crown on your fair maiden's head!

Play with variations for a fun pattern or texture, such as covering the entire crown with glitter or using strips of fabric instead of newsprint.

FAIR MAIDEN WAND

Make this magic wand in an afternoon with simple materials you're sure to have on hand.

MATERIALS

Pencil

Brown paper bag

Scissors

Sewing machine

Thread to match craft paint color

Small foam brush

Acrylic craft paint in a color of your choice

Wooden dowel ¼-inch (6-mm) in diameter, cut to approximately 20 inches (51 cm)

Fiberfill or other stuffing

Hot glue gun

Hot glue sticks

Craft glue

Glitter

1 Photocopy or scan and print the star template (see pullout sheet inside back cover) at 100%. Cut out the template. Using a pencil, trace around the template onto a brown paper bag. Repeat to make two stars. Cut out the stars.

2 Using your sewing machine and thread to match your paint color, stitch around all sides of the star, leaving an opening at the bottom.

3 Using a small foam brush, paint both sides of the paper star. Paint the wooden dowel the same color. Set aside to dry.

4 Stuff the painted star with a small amount of stuffing (enough to give it a bit of dimension).

5 Place a dab of hot glue on the tip of the dowel and insert the dowel into the opening in the bottom of the star.

6 Seal the opening of the star around the dowel with hot glue. Let the glue dry.

7 Brush the star with a thin layer of craft glue. Sprinkle glitter evenly over the star. Let the glue dry, then repeat with the second side of the star.

8 Your wand is now ready for your fair maiden!

TIP
Encourage your fair maiden to decorate her new wand with fun accessories, such as flowing ribbons!

KNIGHTS AND NOBLES TABLE TENT

Spend countless hours dreaming up dragons and grand quests in this private table tent.

MATERIALS

6¼ yards (5.7 m) of 45-inch (114-cm) white cotton or canvas

4½ yards (4.1 m) of 45-inch (114-cm) assorted colorful fabrics for tent lining

Straight pins

Cotton thread in white

Iron

One 9-by-12-inch (23-by-30-cm) sheet of red felt

Scrap for flag

Standard rectangular dining table approximately 60 by 36 inches (152 by 91 cm) on top and 28 inches (71 cm) high

Drill

⅝-inch (15.5mm or 16mm) drill bit

One wood block, 1¾ inch (4.5 cm) square and 4 inches (10 cm) long

Fine sandpaper

½-inch (1.3-cm) dowel for flag

Eighteen 6-by-12-inch (15-by-30-cm) assorted fabric pieces for bunting

2 yards (1.8 m) extra-wide (½ inch/ 1.3 cm) double-fold bias tape

Safety pins or Velcro, to attach bunting to tent

TENT

1 Cut the white cotton to the measurements given on page 54 **(A)**, making one of piece A and two each of pieces C, D, E, and F. Use the pattern template (see pullout pattern sheet inside back cover) for piece B, copying it at 100%.

2 Repeat step 1 to cut the lining fabric pieces for B, C, D, and E. (You do not need lining for pieces A or F.)

3 For piece B, first cut fourteen 1½-inch (4-cm) equilateral triangles out of red felt. Place the triangles along the curve of the canvas piece B with points facing inward, and then place the lining piece B right side down over the top, sandwiching the triangles between the canvas and the lining. Pin the layers together. Using a ¼-inch (6-mm) seam allowance, sew the canvas and lining together, making sure to sew the triangles in place and leaving the long, straight edge open **(B)**. Turn right side out and press.

4 For pieces C, D, and E, with right sides together, pin and sew the canvas and lining fabric together, leaving the top side open **(C)**. Turn right side out and press. Set aside.

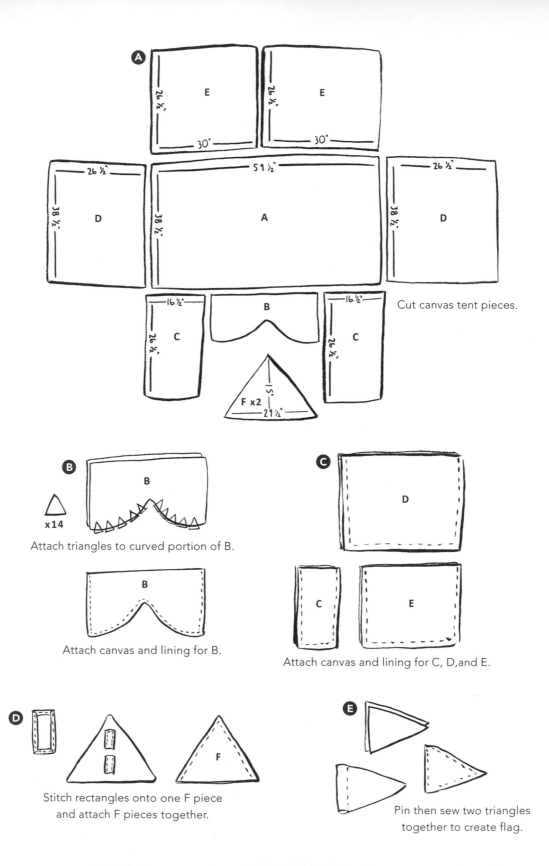

A

E
26 ½"
30"

E
26 ½"
30"

D
26 ½"
38 ½"

A
59 ½"
38 ½"

D
26 ½"
38 ½"

Cut canvas tent pieces.

C
16 ½"
26 ½"

B

C
16 ½"
26 ½"

F x2
15"
21 ½"

B

x14

B

Attach triangles to curved portion of B.

B

Attach canvas and lining for B.

C

D

C

E

Attach canvas and lining for C, D, and E.

D

F

Stitch rectangles onto one F piece
and attach F pieces together.

E

Pin then sew two triangles
together to create flag.

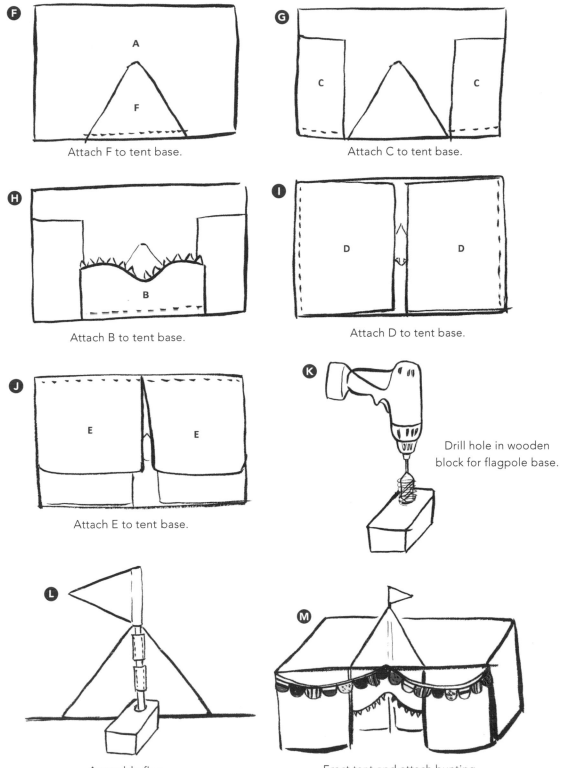

F Attach F to tent base.

G Attach C to tent base.

H Attach B to tent base.

I Attach D to tent base.

J Attach E to tent base.

K Drill hole in wooden block for flagpole base.

L Assemble flag.

M Erect tent and attach bunting.

5 For piece F, first cut two 2¼-by-5¼-inch (6-by-13.5-cm) rectangles out of white canvas. Turn the edges of one rectangle under ¼ inch (6 mm) on each side, press, and sew the turned edge. Repeat for the second rectangle. Stitch the long sides of both rectangles onto the middle of one right side of piece F. Pin both F pieces together, right sides facing. Using a ¼-inch (6-mm) seam allowance, stitch along the edges, leaving the lower edge open **(D)**. Turn right side out and press.

6 Cut two long triangles of equal size out of scrap fabric for the tent flag. Pin the pieces with right sides together, and then stitch all the way around, leaving an opening of a little over an inch (2.5 cm) at the bottom **(E)**. Turn right side out and press.

7 Stitch about an inch (2.5 cm) away from the short end of the triangle. Place dowel inside the newly sewn sleeve.

8 Center piece F over piece A **(F)**; the right side of piece A should be facing the side of piece F to which you attached the rectangles in step 5. Pin and stitch along the long edge of piece F.

9 With right sides facing, pin both C panels to piece A on either side of piece B **(G)**. Using a ½-inch (1.3-cm) seam allowance, stitch both C panels in place along their short bottom edges.

10 Center piece B over piece of F, lining side up **(H)**; pin, and using a ½-inch (1.3-cm) seam allowance, stitch along the long edge of piece B.

11 With right sides facing, pin both D panels to piece A on either short end **(I)**. Using a ½-inch (1.3-cm) seam allowance, stitch both D panels in place along their long outer edges.

12 With right sides facing, pin both E panels to piece A on the long side opposite piece B **(J)**. Using a ½-inch (1.3-cm) seam allowance, stitch both E panels in place along the top edge.

13 Serge (or zigzag stitch) all around the outer edge (be careful not to catch any of the hanging panel fabric in the hem).

14 Turn the tent right side out and press.

15 Set the tent over a rectangular table with piece B facing front and all the panels hanging over the edges of the table.

16 Using a drill and the drill bit, make a hole 1¼ inch (3 cm) deep in the wooden block **(K)**. Sand the block and set it on the table so it is perpendicular to piece F.

17 Place the dowel through the rectangles on the back side of triangle F and insert the end of the dowel into the hole you drilled in the wooden block, so that triangle F stands up straight, topped with the flag **(L)**.

BUNTING

1 Fold each piece of fabric for the bunting in half lengthwise and cut out two scallop shapes using the scallop template on page 130.

2 With right sides facing, pin the two pieces for each scallop together. Using a ¼-inch (6-mm) seam allowance, stitch around the curved edge, leaving the top straight edge open. Turn right side out and press. Repeat for the remaining seventeen scallops.

3 Sandwich the scallops side-by-side between the folds of the bias tape and pin. Stitch together. Turn the ends of the bias tape under about ½-inch (1.3-cm) and stitch.

4 Attach the bunting to the tent with safety pins or velcro. **(M)**

TIP
To change the look of your tent for different parties, simply sew up new bunting based on each event's themes and colors.

TWIG CROWN

Have fun taking your little one on a nature walk
to collect the twigs for this crown!

MATERIALS

Measuring tape

Poster board

Scissors

Hot glue gun

Hot glue sticks

Large pile twigs broken
into pieces between 9 and 12
inches (23 and 30 cm) long

Paintbrush (optional)

Acrylic paint or spray paint
in mint green or a color of
your choice

1 Measure the circumference of your child's head and add 4 inches (10 cm) to that number. Cut a strip of poster board to that length and trim it so it is 6 inches (15 cm) tall (A).

2 Overlap the short edges of the poster board strip by 2 inches (5 cm) (B). Hot-glue the overlapping edges together, creating a cylinder shape. The cylinder should fit snugly around your child's head.

3 Using hot glue, glue the twigs around the poster board cylinder, attaching them one at a time until the crown is completely covered (C).

4 Using a paintbrush, cover the twigs completely with mint green paint. (Alternatively, an adult can spray paint the twigs on a covered work surface in a well-ventilated area.) Let dry completely.

5 Your crown is now ready to wear—encourage a woodland world of make-believe!

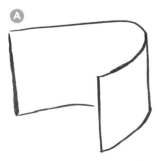

Cut strip of poster board.

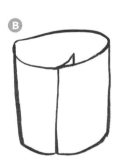

Overlap short edges and glue.

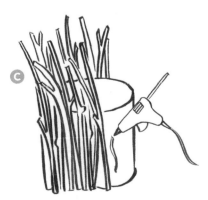

Glue twigs to poster board.

WOODEN DOLL-FACE NECKLACES

Let your little ones express themselves by customizing these precious necklaces. Have fun picking out different hair colors and bun styles, or match your child's hairstyle for a mini self-portrait!

MATERIALS

Wooden disc 2 inches (5 cm) in diameter from craft store

Pencil

Drill

1/16-inch (1.6mm) drill bit

One or two 1½-inch (4-cm) wooden beads, for buns

Paintbrush

Acrylic craft paint in colors of your choice

Small dishes or cups for holding paint

Beeswax polish

One or two 18-inch (46-cm) strings or ribbons

1 Lightly sketch hair and eyes onto your wooden disc with a pencil.

2 Mark the placement of the buns on the disc with a pencil. For a single top bun, mark the center top of the disc, ½ inch (1.3 cm) from the edge of the disc. For two side buns, mark 1¼ inches (3 cm) from the center top on each side, ¼ inch (6 mm) from the edge of the disc; then make a second mark about ¾ inch (2 cm) from the first mark on each side **(A)**.

3 Drill a small hole through the disc at each bun placement marking **(B)**.

4 Paint hair in the color of your choice directly on the wooden disc and paint the bun beads in the same color. Paint two small dots for eyes **(C)**. Let the paint dry.

5 Apply a layer of beeswax polish over the disc and bun beads to protect the paint.

6 Assemble the necklace: For a doll with one bun, simply draw one end of a string or ribbon through the center hole, draw both ends up through the wooden bead, and tie a knot above the bead **(D)**. Tie the string or ribbon ends together **(F)**.

For a doll with two buns, you will need two ribbons. Beginning on one side, draw the end of the first string through each hole from the back side of the disc. Bring both ends together and draw them

through the wooden bead, and tie a knot above the bead. Repeat this process for the other side **(E)**. Tie the ends of the left side to the ends of the right side **(F)**.

7 Your necklace is now ready to wear!

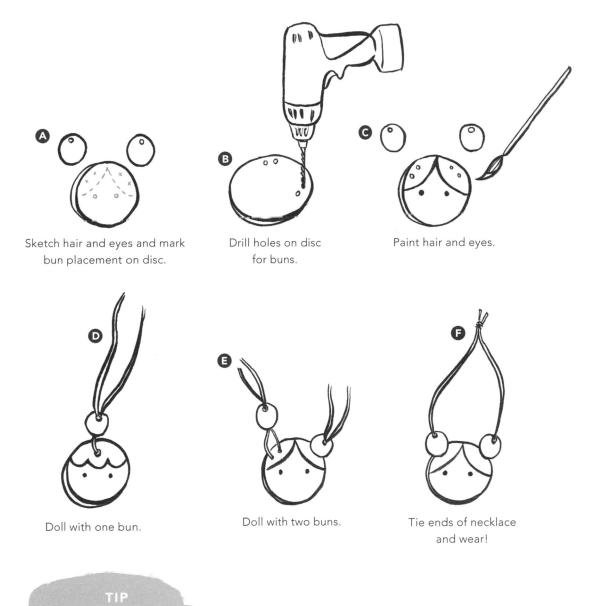

Sketch hair and eyes and mark bun placement on disc.

Drill holes on disc for buns.

Paint hair and eyes.

Doll with one bun.

Doll with two buns.

Tie ends of necklace and wear!

TIP
Add cheeks, a smile, a bow below the bun, or more!

PLAYFUL TOYS

SOFT TRAPEZE DOLL

Take your little one on a playful journey worthy
of the big top with this little performer!

MATERIALS

Two 8½-by-11-inch (22-by-28-cm)
printable canvas sheets

Fabric scissors

All-purpose scissors

2 fat quarters (18-by-22-inch/46-
by-56-cm) fabric pieces in different
colors or prints, for arms and legs

Straight pins

Sewing machine

Thread in a color to match fabrics

Fiberfill or other stuffing

Iron

Two 12-inch (30-cm) pieces 10-
gauge (2.59 mm) artistic wire

1 Scan and print out the templates for the doll face and your choice of bodice from pages 132 to 135 onto printable canvas sheets at 100%. Cut out the pieces with fabric scissors **(A)**.

2 Photocopy the arm and leg templates (see pullout sheet inside back cover) at 100% and cut them out with scissors.

3 With right sides together, stitch the front head piece to the front bodice piece. Repeat for the back head piece and back bodice piece **(B)**.

4 Fold the arm fabric in half and then in half again. Pin the arm pattern piece to the fabric. Cut around the pattern piece to make four arm pieces. Repeat with the leg fabric and pattern piece to make four leg pieces **(C)**.

5 With right sides facing, stitch two arm pieces together, leaving an opening at the flat end. Repeat with the remaining arm pieces and the leg pieces **(D)**. Turn the arms and legs right sides out. Stuff them firmly with fiberfill **(E)**.

6 Place the front head and bodice piece and the back head and bodice piece together, right sides facing. Pin the arms between the bodice pieces, pinning one arm on each side and aligning the flat edge of each arm with the bodice edge. Stitch all the way around, leaving an opening at the bottom of the bodice **(F)**. Turn the doll torso right side out.

7 Turn the lower edge of the bodice under ¼ inch (6 mm) and press with the iron. Stuff the bodice **(G)**.

8 Fold each end of the wire pieces back onto itself ½ inch (1 cm) and twist the folded sections. Place one piece of wire into the center of each stuffed leg **(H)**.

Cut out doll face and
bodice pieces.

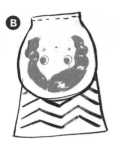

Stitch front head piece to
front bodice piece.

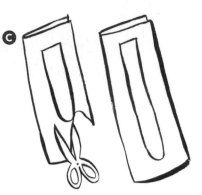

Cut out arm and leg pieces.

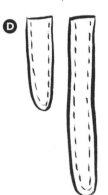

Stitch together fronts and
backs of arm and leg pieces.

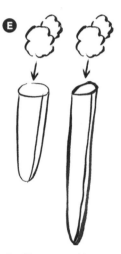

Stuff arms and legs.

Assemble and sew head and
bodice piece and arms.

Stuff bodice.

Insert cut wire into
each stuffed leg.

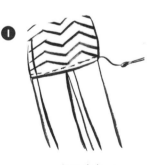

Attach legs.

9 Pin the legs inside the bodice and stitch across the bottom edge of the bodice to attach the legs. **(I)**

TIP: For extra fun, make a simple skirt or ruffled collar for your trapeze doll (or use leftover scraps or rickrack to make a headband!). To make a skirt, cut or rip a piece of stiff cotton organdy into an 8-by-45-inch (20-by-114-cm) strip. With right sides together, fold the fabric in half widthwise. Pin and stitch using a ¼-inch (6-mm) seam allowance to create a tube. With wrong sides together, fold the top of the tube down, matching raw edges together, to create a double-layered tube. Stitch ⅛ inch (3 mm) from the folded edge, around the perimeter of the tube. Stitch a scant ⅜ inch (1 cm) from the first row of stitching to create a casing, leaving a 1-inch (2.5-cm) opening. Thread a 6½-inch (16.5-cm) piece of ⅛-inch (3-mm) elastic through the casing, leaving the ends out. Overlap the ends of the elastic ½ inch (1 cm), and stitch them together. Stitch the opening in the casing closed.

To make the collar, cut or rip a piece of stiff cotton organdy into a 3-by-30-inch (8-by-76-cm) strip. Fold one long edge of fabric ¼ inch (6 mm) toward the wrong side. Press the fold. Pin an approximately 30-inch (76-cm) strip of mini pom-pom or other trim to the folded edge on the wrong side and edge stitch along the fold. With right sides together, fold the fabric in half widthwise. Pin and stitch using a ¼-inch (6-mm) seam allowance to create a tube. Fold the unfinished edge down ⅝ inch (1.5 cm) toward the wrong side. Stitch as close to the edge of the fold as possible, around the perimeter of the tube. Stitch ¼ inch (6 mm) from the first row of stitching to create a casing, leaving a 1-inch (2.5-cm) opening to thread elastic through. Thread a 6½-inch (16.5-cm) piece of ⅛-inch (3-mm) elastic through the casing, leaving the ends out. Overlap the ends of the elastic ½ inch (1 cm), and stitch them together. Stitch the opening in the casing closed.

TIERED STACKING ANIMAL BLOCKS

Help your preschooler learn about animals
and proportion while playing with these cute blocks.

MATERIALS

Chop saw

One piece wood 2½ inches
(6.5 cm) square and at least
30 inches (76 cm) long

Sandpaper

Soft graphite pencil

Bone folder or spoon

Acrylic paints in black, red,
white, blue, light blue,
orange, pink, and gray, or
colors of your choice

Paintbrush

Beeswax polish

1 Using the saw, cut the wood into pieces of the following lengths: 6 inches (15 cm), 5½ inches (14 cm), 5 inches (13 cm), 4½ inches (11.5 cm), 4 inches (10 cm) (A).

2 Sand the rough edges of the wooden blocks (B).

3 Photocopy the animal templates on pages 130 and 131 at 100%.

4 Trace over the lines of each animal template with the pencil, pressing firmly (C). Cut out the templates and label them on the blank side with the size of their corresponding block.

5 For each animal block, turn the paper over so that the graphite drawing is facedown over the corresponding size block.

6 Using a bone folder or the back of a spoon, firmly rub the surface of the paper in a back-and-forth motion, being sure to go over the entire drawing (D). This will transfer the drawing of the animal onto the block of wood.

7 Repeat step 6 until all five drawings have been transferred to their corresponding blocks.

8 Following the lines of the transferred animal templates, paint each block, using the project photo on the opposite page as a guide, if desired (E).

9 Once you have painted your entire animal, you can then go back with a thin brush and subtly outline a few areas with black paint to define the animal even more, if desired. Let the paint dry.

10 Following the manufacturer's instructions, seal the blocks with beeswax polish for additional protection. Let the blocks dry.

11 The animal blocks are now ready for your little ones to play with! Have fun helping your children learn as they stack the animals on top of one another.

A

Cut wooden block into five sizes for stacking.

B

Sand edges of each block.

C

Trace over animal templates.

D

Rub back side of paper to transfer image.

E

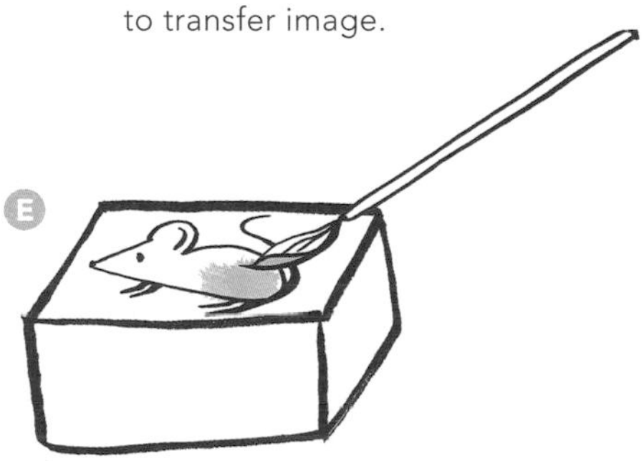

Paint blocks.

TIP

Paint the names of the animals on the back sides of the blocks for a great early reading activity!

SQUIGGLE FLOOR TILE PUZZLE

Entertain your little one for hours with this fun floor puzzle!
Match up the colors to make circles or just go for a
freestyle squiggle approach—the simple half-circle shapes
on each tile make for an endless number of combinations.

MATERIALS

Three 12-inch (30-cm) squares of
⅛-inch (3-mm) craft plywood (I found
mine at my local craft store)

Table saw

Pencil

Sandpaper

Acrylic craft paint in at least 5
assorted colors (I used red, white,
blue, yellow, and black)

1¼-inch (3-cm) sponge brush

Beeswax polish

1 Using a saw, cut each sheet of craft plywood down the middle both ways to make four equal-size square tiles (**A**). (You can actually cut any size tiles you want—they just need to be square, and the size of the quarter-circle template will have to be adjusted proportionately.)

2 Sand the edges of each tile (**B**).

3 Photocopy and cut out the quarter-circle template (see pullout sheet inside back cover) at 100%. Cut out the quarter-circle shape.

4 Lay the stencil on a plywood tile so the flat edges are flush against the two sides of the tile. Using a pencil, trace the shape onto the tile. Repeat this step on the opposite corner of the tile (**C**).

5 Lay your tiles down in a grid.

6 Using acrylic craft paint and a sponge brush, fill in the outlines, following **D** for reference (from left to right):

TILE 1: red, white	**TILE 7:** blue, red
TILE 2: white, blue	**TILE 8:** red, yellow
TILE 3: blue, white	**TILE 9:** red, black
TILE 4: white, yellow	**TILE 10:** black, yellow
TILE 5: red, black	**TILE 11:** yellow, red
TILE 6: black, blue	**TILE 12:** red, black

7 After the paint has dried, apply a coat of beeswax polish to set the paint and to help avoid nicks and scrapes.

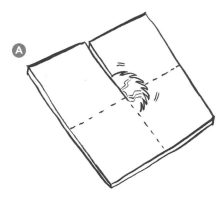

Cut four equal-sized square tiles from plywood.

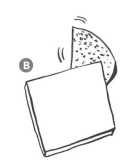

Sand edges of each tile.

Trace quarter-circle shape onto tile corners.

Paint within outlines.

TIP
Paint the back sides of the tiles with triangle shapes for two puzzles in one!

WOODEN PLAY VILLAGE

Your little one will be lost in hours of play with this community play set, complete with buildings, cars, peg people, and a floor mat.

MATERIALS

BASIC TOOLS

Pencil

Ruler

Drill

1-inch (25.5-mm) drill bit

13/64-inch (5.2-mm) drill bit

3/16-inch (4.7-mm) drill bit

Chop saw

Sandpaper

Newsprint

Painter's tape (optional)

Acrylic craft paints in a variety of colors, including black, turquoise, and red

Paintbrush

Glue

Beeswax polish

3½-inch (9-cm) paint roller

Fabric scissors

Sewing pins

Hand-sewing needle or sewing machine

WOODEN VEHICLES AND PEG PEOPLE

Three 1¾-inch (4.5-cm) square wooden blocks cut 4 inches (13 cm) long (I found mine precut to this size at local craft store) (for cars)

One 1¾-inch (4.5-mm) square wooden block cut 5 inches (13 cm) long (for boat)

One 1-by-26-inch (2.5-by-66-cm) wooden dowel

One 3/8-by-26-inch (1-by-66-cm) wooden dowel

Set of twelve 1½-inch (6-cm) wooden wheels

Set of twelve ¼-inch (6-mm) thick wooden axles

8-inch (20-cm) canvas square (for boat sail)

WOODEN HOUSES AND TREE

One 3-foot (1-m) piece 2-by-6-inch (5-by-15-cm) wooden board (for houses)

One 12-inch (30-cm) piece 2-by-4-inch (5-by-10-cm) wooden board (for tree)

PLAY MAT

40-inch (1-m) square canvas (for play mat)

40-inch (1-m) square batting (for play mat)

40-inch (1-m) square backing fabric (for play mat)

3 yards (2.8 m) 7/8-inch (2.2-cm) double-fold bias tape or quilt binding

Thread in a color corresponding to bias tape

A

Drill holes for wheel axles on long sides of car block.

B

Drill one or two equal-sized holes on top of car block.

C

Drill two holes of different sizes on top of boat block.

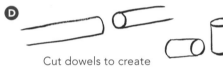

D

Cut dowels to create peg people.

E

Paint peg people.

F

Paint car.

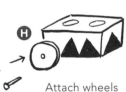

G

Paint boat.

H

Attach wheels to block.

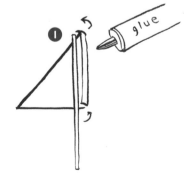

I

Glue flag to dowel.

J

Stand flag in smaller drilled hole in boat.

WOODEN VEHICLES AND PEG PEOPLE

1 For each side of the car, mark two holes 2 inches (5 cm) apart and ⅝ inch (1.6 cm) from the bottom edge of the block, making sure they are at the same height. Using a drill with a ³/₁₆-inch (4.7-mm) drill bit, drill four ¾-inch (2-cm) deep holes at the marks for the wheel axles **(A)**.

2 Using a 1-inch (25.5-mm) drill bit, drill one or two holes ¾ inch (2 cm) deep in the top of each car block **(B)**. Drill one hole ¾ inch (2 cm) deep toward one side of the top of the boat block **(C)**.

3 Using a ¹³/₆₄-inch (5.2-mm) drill bit, drill one hole 1 inch (2.5 cm) deep in the other side of the top of the boat **(C)**.

4 Cut at least four 2¼-inch (6-cm) long pieces from the larger dowel. (If you want extra characters, cut more.) Cut one 3½-inch (9-cm) long piece—this will be the character with the top hat **(D)**.

5 Sand the rough edges of the dowels and the wooden blocks.

6 Stand the dowels on end and place the blocks lengthwise on a piece of newsprint.

7 Using a paintbrush and the colors of your choice, paint simple eyes, hair, and clothing patterns on the dowels **(E)**. Paint simple designs on the sides of each car **(F)**. Paint the sides of the boat **(G)**. Use painter's tape to tape off sections for a clean line, or just eyeball it. Paint the wheels. Let all the pieces dry.

8 Insert the axles into the holes in the base of the cars and attach one wheel to each axle with a dab of glue to secure **(H)**.

9 For the boat sail, cut the smaller dowel down to 8¼ inches (21 cm).

10 Cut a triangle out of canvas and wrap one end around the dowel. Glue it in place **(I)**. Stand the boat flag in the small hole you drilled in the boat **(J)**.

11 Following the manufacturer's instructions, use beeswax polish to seal the cars, boat, and people.

WOODEN BUILDINGS AND TREE

❶ From the larger board, use your chop saw to cut the following pieces:

SHOP BUILDING: 5½-by-6-inch (14-by-15-cm) block

TREE: 4-by-6-inch (10-by-15cm) block

PEAKED HOUSES: Decide the height you want for your peaked house. Mark this measurement on the board **(K)**. Set your chop saw at a 45-degree angle and cut on both sides, meeting at the middle of the board, to create the angled roof. Repeat to make a second house.

❷ Sand each piece of wood.

❸ Paint roofs, windows, doors, and the tree onto the blocks of wood, following the project photograph as a guide, if desired **(L)**. Let dry.

❹ Following the manufacturer's instructions, use the beeswax polish to finish the houses and tree.

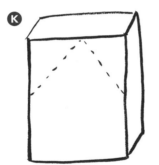

Mark and cut boards to
create angled roof.

Paint house details.

Paint road pattern and
waves on canvas.

Stack backing, batting,
and painted canvas.

Pin and sew together.

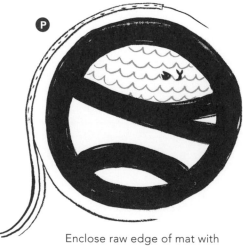

Enclose raw edge of mat with
binding tape; pin and sew.

PLAY MAT

❶ Measure and mark a circle with a 38-inch (9-cm) diameter on the canvas, batting, and backing fabric pieces. Cut out the circle from each piece.

❷ Using a paint roller and black paint, paint on a road pattern for your cars on the canvas, following the project photograph, if desired **(M)**. Leave spaces for the houses and tree to stand and for a lake. Paint waves in the lake, and, if you'd like, add a fish. Let dry.

❸ Place the backing fabric right side down on your work surface, top it with the batting, and finally place the canvas painted side up over the batting **(N)**. Using a ½-inch (1.3-cm) seam allowance, pin and sew the three fabric layers together **(O)**.

❹ Enclose the raw edge of the play mat with double-fold bias tape and pin it in place. Sew the binding tape to the play mat, being sure to keep the raw edge in the tape **(P)**.

WOODEN ANIMAL MOBILE

Your little one will be delighted by this simple
and easy-to-make modern mobile.

MATERIALS

Two 12-inch (30-cm) squares ⅛-inch (3-mm) craft plywood (I found mine at my local craft store)

Scroll saw

Sandpaper

Scissors

Pencil

Beeswax polish

Acrylic craft paints in a few colors

Paintbrush

Drill

⁵⁄₆₄-inch (2-mm) drill bit

Wood glue

Fishing line

Ceiling hook

1. Cut two 1½-by-12-inch (4-by-30-cm) strips from the craft plywood with the scroll saw (A).

2. Cut ½-inch (1.3-cm) slots in the middle of each plywood strip (B).

3. Sand the strips and interlock them at the slots. Set aside.

4. Photocopy or scan and print the mobile templates (see pullout sheet inside back cover) at 100%. Cut out the shapes. Trace all the animal shapes, bodies, and legs onto craft plywood (C). Mark the slots and drill holes as they are indicated on the templates.

5. Cut out the animal shapes with the scroll saw.

6. Cut out the marked slots in the animal bodies and legs of the giraffe, horse, and pig.

7. Sand all pieces of plywood. Polish the pieces using all-natural beeswax polish, following the manufacturer's instructions.

8. Paint the animal legs, elephant ears, and bird wings a solid color of your choosing using acrylic craft paints (D). Let dry.

9. Using the templates as a guide, drill a hole in each animal body (E).

10. Assemble the animal shapes, dabbing a bit of wood glue on and around the interlocking slots of each piece and then inserting the corresponding legs, wings, and ears into the appropriate animal body (F). Hold firmly for a few seconds, then set aside and let dry completely.

A

Cut two strips from plywood.

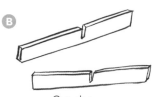

B

Cut slots.

C

Trace shapes onto plywood.

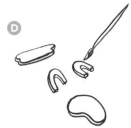

D

Paint legs and wings.

E

Drill hole in each
body shape.

F

Assemble and glue
interlocking slots.

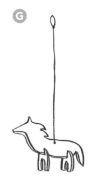

G

Tie fishing line
through drilled hole.

H

Assemble mobile.

I

Hang mobile from ceiling hook.

11 Cut the fishing line into varying lengths, between 5 and 12 inches (13 and 30 cm) long. Tie one length of fishing line through the drilled hole in each animal, making sure each string is knotted securely (G).

12 Tie the fishing line attached to each animal to the strips of plywood, making sure the strings are secure. Start by tying the bird to the crossed center of the interlocking strips.The giraffe and the elephant, being the heaviest animals, will need to be placed about 6 inches (15 cm) in from the edge of the plywood strip. The horse and the pig will need to be placed about 1½ inches (4 cm) in from the edge (H). Adjust the positions of the animals until you are satisfied with how the mobile is balanced.

13 Screw a ceiling hook into the ceiling, making sure it is secure.

14 Cut a piece of fishing line to the length of your choosing. Tie it securely to the center of the mobile, over and around the interlocking center.

15 Tie a loop at the top of the fishing line, making sure it is secure, then place the loop over the ceiling hook (I). Be sure the mobile is securely attached to both the center and the hook to avoid any risk of falling.

PLAYFUL ART

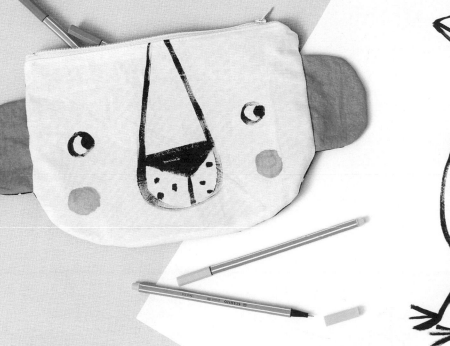

ANIMAL ART

There are so many fun ways you can use these three animal friends. Create animal posters, pillows, and more for your little one to color and enjoy!

PRINTS

These make great art for the kiddo's room!

16-by-20-inch (41-by-51-cm) or smaller matte cardstock

Markers, crayons, or colored pencils (optional)

1 To make poster prints, simply photocopy or scan and print the lion, rabbit, and/or bird art on pages 136 to 138 onto matte cardstock.

2 Hang the prints as they are, or have your child color them in with markers, crayons, or colored pencils.

PILLOWS

You can also print these animal friends onto printable fabric to make your very own custom softies. Determine the amount of fabric you need based on the pillow size desired.

Printable fabric (I prefer canvas for its durability)

Fabric in contrasting color

Hand-sewing needle or sewing machine

Thread in a neutral or complementary color

Fabric scissors

Fiberfill or other stuffing

Fabric paint or markers (optional)

1 Scan the lion, rabbit, and/or bird art on pages 136 to 138.

2 Decide what size you want your pillow to be and enlarge the art accordingly. Follow the manufacturer's instructions for printing the animal art onto the printable fabric.

3 Cut the contrasting fabric to match the size of the printed fabric.

4 Pin the printed fabric and contrasting fabric with right sides together **(A)**.

5 Using a hand-sewing needle and thread or a sewing machine, stitch around the animal design however you would like, staying at least 1 inch (2.5 cm) away from the artwork and leaving about a 2½-inch (6-cm) opening on one side to insert the fiberfill **(B)**.

6 Trim excess fabric **(C)**.

7 Turn the pillowcase right side out through the opening.

8 Stuff the pillow, using small handfuls to prevent lumpiness, until you are happy with how taut it is **(D)**.

9 Hand-sew the opening closed.

10 Add a touch of color with fabric paint or markers.

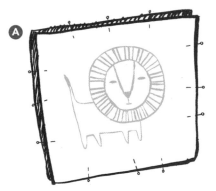

Pin printed and backing fabric with right sides facing.

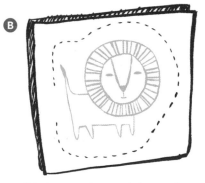

Stitch around animal design, leaving small opening for stuffing later.

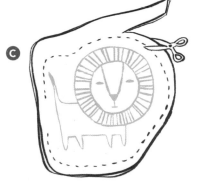

Trim excess fabric.

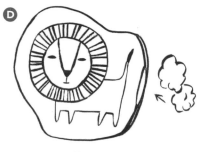

Stuff pillow.

PENCIL BAGS

Carry your art supplies in your
very own custom bag.

MATERIALS

1 fat quarter (18-by-22-inch/
46-by-56-cm piece) cotton or
linen, for the outside of bag

1 fat quarter (18-by-22-inch/
46-by-56-cm piece) cotton,
for lining bag

All-purpose scissors

Straight pins

Fabric scissors

Fabric paints

Paintbrush

7-inch (18-cm) standard zipper

Sewing machine with zipper
foot

Thread to match outer fabric

Iron and ironing board

MAKE THE BAG

1 If you are making the bear face bag, photocopy or scan and print the bear face bag and ear templates (see pullout sheet inside back cover) at 100%. If you are making the rectangular bag, create a rectangular template measuring 8 by 10¾ inches (20 by 27 cm). Cut out the outer and lining pattern pieces and ear pieces, if using.

2 Fold the outer fabric in half. Pin the outer pattern piece to the fabric. Using fabric scissors and following the pattern, cut out to create two pieces. Repeat with the lining fabric and lining pattern piece. If you are making a bear-face bag, fold a 14-inch (36-cm) piece of the outer fabric and an equal-size piece of the lining fabric and place them with folded edges aligned. Pin the ear pattern to the four layers of fabric and cut out two outer and two lining pieces for the ears (A).

3 Using fabric paint, paint designs or a bear face (freehand or following the template on page 139) onto the right side of one outer fabric piece. Let the paint dry (B).

4 Place one lining piece right side up on your work surface. Place the zipper facedown on the lining piece, aligning it with the edge where the bag will open. Place one outer piece right side down over the zipper and lining, aligning its edge with the edge of the zipper and lining fabric (C). Pin the three layers together.

5 Using a sewing machine with the zipper foot and thread to match the outer fabric, sew across the top edge (D).

A — Cut out pattern pieces in lining and outer fabric.

B — Paint design or bear face.

C — Pin lining and outer fabric to one edge of zipper.

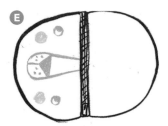

D — Sew across top edge.

E — Repeat with remaining lining and outer fabric on free edge of zipper.

F — Sew ears.

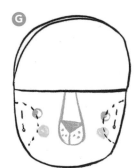

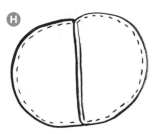

G — Separate fabrics and pin ears between outer pieces.

H — Sew bag edges.

I — Turn right side out through zipper opening.

J — Tuck in lining.

K — Fill bag and enjoy!

6 Repeat steps 4 and 5 with the free side of the zipper and the second outer and lining fabric pieces. Using an iron and ironing board, press all the seams (E).

7 For a bear-face bag, place one outer and one lining ear piece with right sides together and pin. Sew around the curved edge of the ear, leaving the straight edge open. Repeat to make a second ear. Turn the ears right side out and press (F).

8 Bring both lining pieces to one side of the zipper and both outer fabric pieces to the other side.

9 Sandwich the ears between the outer fabric pieces, with the rounded edge facing in and the flat edge aligned to the edges of the outer fabric. Pin the edges, making sure to catch the ears between the fabric layers (G).

10 Unzip the zipper about halfway so you will be able to turn the bag right side out once it has been stitched.

11 Leaving the zipper halfway open, sew all the way around the edge of the bag with a ¼-inch (6-mm) seam allowance (H).

12 Clip the corners.

13 Turn the bag right side out through the zipper (I).

14 Tuck the lining into the bag (J).

15 You are finished! Place pencils or other items in your bag, and enjoy (K)!

TIP
Have your child paint his or her own designs or bear face onto the bag for a truly kid-custom creation.

FINGERPRINT ART

Capture this special time in your child's life with these darling fingerprint rain cloud and flower stalk works of art.

MATERIALS

One 11-by-14-inch (28-by-36-cm) sheet cardstock or watercolor paper

Child-safe inkpads in the colors of your choice

11-by-14-inch (28-by-36-cm) frame or colorful tape (optional)

1 Photocopy or scan and print the cloud or flower stalk artwork on pages 140 and 141, printing the image in color onto cardstock or watercolor paper at whatever size you like. To make the size shown, enlarge the artwork by 125%.

2 Have your child press his or her thumb on an inkpad, then leave a print on the paper, creating rows of raindrops or flowers. If you have more than one child, you can differentiate the colors of the raindrops slightly for easy identification.

3 Once the ink is dry, frame the fingerprinted paper or tape it to your wall with fun, colorful tape. Be sure to record your child's name and age for a lasting memento!

TIP
Ask each student in your child's class to stamp one thumbprint for a great teacher gift!

PENCIL HOLDER HEADS

Hold your favorite pencils with these
silly pencil holder heads.

MATERIALS

3½-inch (9-cm) square
wooden block

Pencil

Ruler

Drill

5/16-inch (8-mm) drill bit (or drill
bit in a size slightly larger than
your writing implement)

Sandpaper

Colorful acrylic craft paints

Paintbrush

Beeswax polish

1 On top of the wooden block, use a pencil and ruler to lightly draw a grid of sixteen squares (A).

2 At each grid intersection, drill straight down about 2 inches (5 cm) into the block (B). Change your drill bit as needed to make smaller or larger holes for smaller or larger writing implements.

3 Sand down the wood block.

4 Now it's time to have fun painting on your very own silly faces! Using acrylic paint and a paintbrush, decorate one (or all four!) sides of the block as desired (C).

5 Finish the pencil holder with beeswax polish, following the manufacturer's instructions.

Draw grid on wooden block.

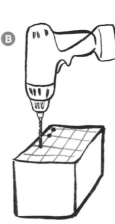

Drill holes.

Paint silly faces.

PLAYFUL
REPURPOSING

TRUK

DUCT TAPE CARDBOARD BROWNSTONE

Look no further than your pantry and supply closet
to make this fun cardboard dollhouse.

MATERIALS

Tall cardboard box (ideally 48 inches/122 cm high, but you can tape together several boxes if you don't have one this tall)

Four 10½-by-11½-inch (26.5-by-29-cm) cardboard pieces for floor

Pencil

Utility knife

Cutting mat

Clear packing tape

Duct tape in a variety of colors

Waxed paper (optional)

Decorative papers for interior of house

Mod Podge

Foam brush

MAKE THE DOLLHOUSE

1 Photocopy and enlarge the building, stoop, and stairs templates (see pullout sheet inside back cover) by 200%. Trace the templates for each house piece onto the cardboard box. Using a utility knife and cutting mat, cut out each piece. Use a pencil to label each piece. The template is given for a stepped roof (A). Adapt it freehand for triangular or curved roof.

2 Cut out the windows and the top, left, and bottom sides of the door. Score the right side of the door so that it can swing open and shut.

3 Begin assembling the dollhouse: Score the sides and roof of the dollhouse at the dashed lines. Turn the cardboard sheet over. Fold the sides of the house back and rooftops together so that they form a peak. Tape the roof together on the inside with packing tape (B).

4 Referring to the marking on the templates, install the four dollhouse floors by taping them to the inside front and sides of the house with packing tape (C).

5 Assemble the stoop: Fold the stair piece where indicated to make stairs, then tape them with packing tape to the stoop sides. Tape on the inside under the stairs so that the packing tape doesn't show (D).

6 Using a contrasting color of duct tape, tape along the top edges of the stoop sides to create stair rails.

7 Tape the stoop to the house with packing tape, taping inside the stairs so that the packing tape doesn't show (E).

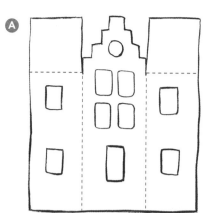

A

Trace template onto
cardboard and cut out.

B

Score and fold sides and
roof. Tape roof from inside.

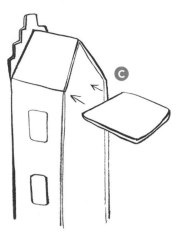

C

Attach floors from inside.

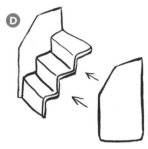

D

Fold stairs and
assemble stoop.

E

Tape stoop to house
frame from inside.

F

Decorate exterior with
duct tape shingles.

G

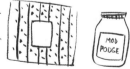

MOD
PODGE

Glue wallpaper to
interior walls.

DECORATE DOLLHOUSE EXTERIOR

1 Choose a contrasting duct tape color for the trim of the house. Run it along the outer edges of the front side of the house as well as along the base of the roof and the base of the house, just above the crawlspace.

2 Outline the trim of the upper roof edge.

3 Trim each window with the color of your choice.

4 Cover the front door piece completely (front and back) in one color. Add a small contrasting circle of tape for the doorknob.

5 Attach the door to the house, taping one side to the inside of the house, using the same color duct tape as you used to cover the door.

6 Now use a variety of colors of duct tape to add decorative elements to the house, such as topiary trees on either side of the stoop.

7 You can also create a brick effect on the lower portion of the crawlspace by cutting thin strips of duct tape and applying them in a brick-like pattern.

8 Create a multicolored pattern on the roof by cutting out shingle shapes in various colors. Rolling out the duct tape on waxed paper and then cutting the shapes makes this easier (F).

DECORATE DOLLHOUSE INTERIOR

1 Cut out interior wallpaper from patterned paper, such as scrapbook paper, based on the dimensions of the rooms in your dollhouse.

2 Using a cutting mat and utility knife, cut out the corresponding window openings in the wallpaper.

3 Apply a generous coat of Mod Podge to the wall, then carefully apply the paper. Smooth the paper from the center out, pressing firmly, to remove any air bubbles (G).

4 Have fun decorating the house interior by adding taped artwork, curtains, furniture, and little friends!

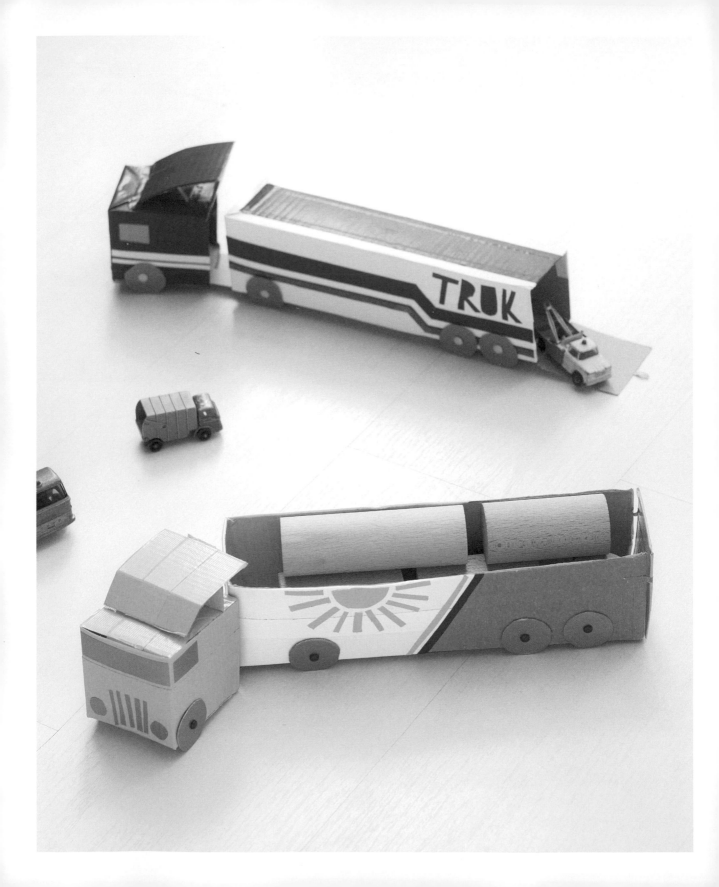

CRACKER BOX TRUCKS

For hours of trucking fun for your little one, look no further than your very own pantry! You can create these diesel rigs in a little less than an afternoon.

MATERIALS

Ruler

Two long, rectangular empty cracker boxes (such as Carr's cracker boxes)

Permanent marker

Scissors

Duct tape in a variety of colors

⅛-inch (3-mm) round hole punch

Pencil or pen

Eight 8mm brads

Waxed paper

1 With a ruler, measure 3 inches (8 cm) from one end of one cracker box and mark this point with a marker. Using scissors, cut crosswise through the box at the point you marked **(A)**. The shorter piece will be the cab of the truck (one end will be closed and the other will be open). Set the longer piece aside.

2 Using scissors, cut off and discard the flaps from the open end of the second cracker box **(B)**. This will be the truck's trailer.

3 Measure the height and width of the trailer opening. Using scissors, cut an equal-size piece from the long scrap section of the first box to make a ramp for the back of the truck. With duct tape in the color of your choice, tape the underside of the ramp to the bottom edge of the opening of the trailer to make a hinge **(C)**.

4 Cut a 2-by-3½-inch (5-by-9-cm) strip from the scraps of the first box. Using a hole punch, punch one hole in each end of the strip about ¼ inch (6 mm) in from the edge. Punch a hole in the bottom of the open end of the truck cab, about ½ inch (1 cm) in from the edge. Using the tip of a pen or a pencil, poke a hole in the bottom of the closed end of the truck trailer, about 1 inch (2.5 cm) in from the edge **(D)**. Use a brad to secure the strip to the bottom of the cab, and a second brad to secure the free end of the strip to the bottom of the trailer **(E)**.

5 Cut eight 1¼-inch (3-cm) circles from the scraps of the first box for wheels. Punch holes in the center of each wheel. Punch or poke corresponding holes in the truck's cab and trailer.

6 Using duct tape in the color of your choice, completely cover the outside of the truck's cab so no cracker box shows through. Repeat with the truck's trailer.

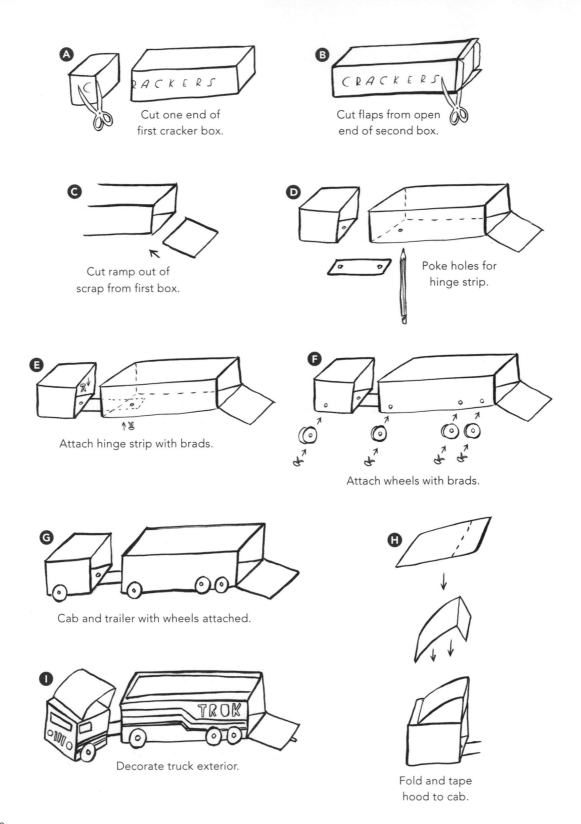

A Cut one end of first cracker box.

B Cut flaps from open end of second box.

C Cut ramp out of scrap from first box.

D Poke holes for hinge strip.

E Attach hinge strip with brads.

F Attach wheels with brads.

G Cab and trailer with wheels attached.

H Fold and tape hood to cab.

I Decorate truck exterior.

7 Cover the wheels with silver or black duct tape, poke center holes through the tape, and attach the wheels to the cab and trailer with brads **(F, G)**.

8 Cut a 4½-inch (11.5-cm) strip the same width as the truck cab from the scraps of the first box to make a hood for the truck cab. Cover the strip with red duct tape. Fold the strip about 3 inches (8 cm) from one end. Use duct tape to adhere it to the center-top of the truck cab **(H)**.

9 On a piece of waxed paper, adhere strips of duct tape in the colors of your choice. Cut out various elements—windows, headlights, words, etc. If you'd like, sketch the shapes on the duct tape in permanent marker before cutting them out. Remove the duct tape shapes from the waxed paper and stick them to the truck **(I)**.

10 Now you are all set to play with your new rig! Place play cars in the truck's trailer for more fun.

TIP
To create a truck bed for hauling twigs, blocks, and more, cut off the top of the truck's trailer.

DUCT TAPE PORTFOLIO

Have your little artist create and customize his or her
very own portfolio out of duct tape!

MATERIALS

Two 12½-by-9½-inch (32-by-24-cm)
pieces cardboard or fiberboard
(such as the front and back of a
large cereal box)

Duct tape in several colors (I used
4 colors for the construction of
the portfolio and an additional
3 colors for the decorative face
on the outside)

Scissors

18-inch (46-cm) ruler

Utility knife

Cutting mat

MAKE PORTFOLIO

1 Lay both boards flat on your work surface, with the long edges side by side, leaving approximately
1 inch (2.5 cm) of space between them (A).

2 Choose the duct tape color you'd like for the portfolio interior. Cut a strip of duct tape long
enough to adhere horizontally across both boards, while maintaining the gap between them.
Continue cutting and adhering strips of duct tape, overlapping them by ¼ inch (6 mm), until the
boards are completely covered.

3 Choose the duct tape color you'd like for the outside of the portfolio. Flip the taped boards over
and cover the untaped side with strips of duct tape as in step 2 (B).

4 Trim any excess tape around the edges of the portfolio (C). (This step can be done with scissors
by a child or an adult, or by an adult using a ruler, utility knife, and cutting mat.)

5 Choose a contrasting duct tape color for the edges of the portfolio. Cut a strip of tape slightly
longer than the length of the portfolio. Place one long edge of the portfolio along the center of the
duct tape strip and fold the strip over to enclose the edge. Trim any excess tape. Repeat with the
remaining sides of the portfolio (D).

6 Cut a 16-inch (41-cm) strip of duct tape in the color of your choice and place it on your work
surface, sticky side up. Cut a second strip the same length and place it directly on top of the first
strip with sticky sides touching. This will be one handle for your portfolio. Repeat to make a second
handle (E).

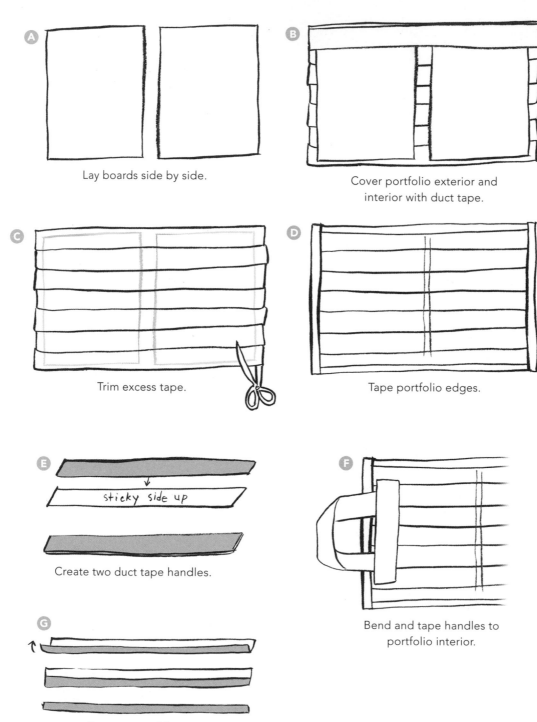

A Lay boards side by side.

B Cover portfolio exterior and interior with duct tape.

C Trim excess tape.

D Tape portfolio edges.

E sticky side up

Create two duct tape handles.

F Bend and tape handles to portfolio interior.

G Create tape ribbons.

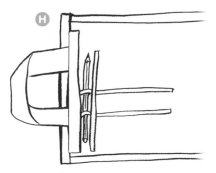

Create pen and pencil slots.

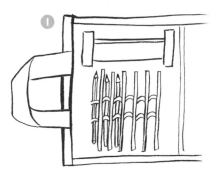

Create and attach small pocket.

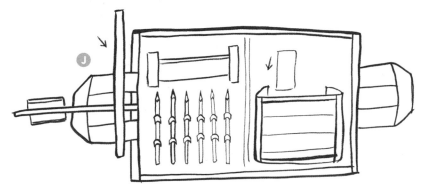

Create and attach large pocket
and portfolio closure.

Decorate exterior.

Adhere closure to keep
your treasures safe!

7 Bend one handle in the middle and tape its ends, spaced 4 inches (10 cm) apart, to the inside of the portfolio, using the same color as the inside of the portfolio (F). Use at least two pieces of duct tape for extra strength. Repeat on the opposite side.

8 Cut a 12-inch (30-cm) strip of duct tape in the same color as the interior of the portfolio. Fold one long edge of the tape down on itself, sticky sides together, then repeat on the other side to form a ribbon of duct tape (G). Repeat with a second piece of tape.

9 Lay both ribbons on the inside of the portfolio where you'd like your pens and pencils to go, leaving 2 inches (5 cm) of space between them. Cut a 5-inch (13-cm) strip of tape in the same color and use it to tape down the ends of both ribbons.

10 Place a pen or pencil underneath the two ribbons and measure approximately how much room you want for each pen; the pen should be held securely in place. Cut a ⅜-by-5-inch (1-by-13-cm) strip of tape and place it alongside the pen over both ribbons (H). Place a second pen under the free side of the ribbons, and repeat the process until you have as many slots as you want. Remove the pens.

11 Cut three 8-inch (20-cm) strips of duct tape in the same color. Place one strip horizontally above the top pen loops, one between the top and bottom pen loops, and one below the bottom pen loops, to reinforce them.

12 To create a small pocket, cut two 12-inch (30-cm) strips of duct tape and place them sticky sides together. If you'd like, cut a piece in a contrasting color as well and use it to encase one long edge of the duct tape ribbon. Fold over the bottom edge of the duct tape ribbon by ½ inch (1.3 cm) and adhere it to the portfolio above the pencil loops. Cut two 2-inch (5-cm) pieces of duct tape and use them to attach the sides of the ribbon to the portfolio, leaving the top open (I).

13 To create the large pocket, roll out five 12-inch (30-cm) strips of duct tape. Overlap the long edges of the strips to create a sheet of duct tape. Repeat with five more strips of tape. Place both sheets together, with sticky sides touching.

14 Fold the edges of the pocket over 1 inch (2.5 cm) on all sides. Place the pocket on the portfolio, folded edges down. Using tape in a corresponding color, tape the pocket to the portfolio, leaving the top edge untaped (J). Now your pocket should be able to hold paper or a sketchbook!

15 To create a closure for your portfolio, make a ribbon of duct tape as you did in step 8. Tape a rectangular piece of duct tape to one end, with the long edges folded over slightly. Use a thin strip of duct tape to attach the ribbon's opposite end, taping it to the inside center edge of the portfolio (J).

16 Now that the interior is finished, you can decorate the outside of your portfolio! Make a face, a pattern, or tape on your very own initial (K). Customize it however you like!

17 Your portfolio is now complete—take it out on your next sketching adventure! Just press down the sticky side of the closure to keep everything safe inside (L).

DUCT TAPE BIRD COSTUME

Transform a discarded packing box into a stunning colorful
bird costume with cardboard and duct tape!

MATERIALS

One large heavy-duty rectangular
cardboard box (I used a box that
measured 17 by 22 by 8½ inches
[43 by 56 by 21.5 cm])

Scissors

Utility knife

Cutting mat

Ruler

Heavy-duty cardboard pieces for
head, wings, and tail

Rolls of colorful duct tape in five
colors

Two small wooden dowels (about
⁵⁄₁₆ by 8 inches/1 by 20 cm)

① Using scissors or a utility knife, cutting mat, and ruler, cut the top and bottom flaps off of the cardboard box.

② Photocopy or scan and print the following templates at 100%: bird wing, head, head tuft, beak, tail (see pullout sheet inside back cover). Cut out the template pieces.

③ For the wings, trace the template twice onto cardboard and cut out to make two wings.

④ Cover both wings in duct tape, using five colors and following the project photograph at left for placement.

⑤ Attach a strip of duct tape, sticky side up, to the top of the underside of one wing, leaving half of the sticky portion exposed. Stick the exposed sticky portion to the upper edge of one side of the box to attach the wing. Repeat with the second wing on the opposite side of the box (A, B).

⑥ Using yellow duct tape, start creating feathers: Cut 7-inch (18-cm) strips of duct tape and fold them over themselves crosswise, leaving about 1 inch (2.5 cm) of tape uncovered (you will stick the uncovered tab to the box). Round off the feathers at the folded end with scissors and secure the feather to the outside of the box using the uncovered portion of the duct tape. Continue making and attaching feathers with this technique until the exterior of the box is covered (C, D).

⑦ For the head, trace the template onto a piece of cardboard. Using scissors or a utility knife, cutting mat, and ruler, cut out the head shape. Using a contrasting color of duct tape, cover the edge of the bird's head. From black duct tape, cut out two eyes. From pink duct tape, cut out two cheek circles. From yellow duct tape, cut out feather scallops. Attach the face details to the bird head following the project photo at left and F for placement.

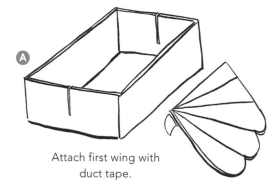

A

Attach first wing with
duct tape.

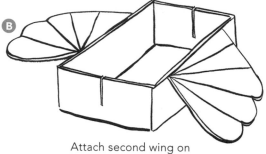

B

Attach second wing on
opposite side.

C

Cut duct tape strip feathers.

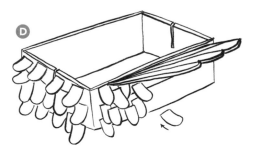

D

Secure feathers to box exterior.

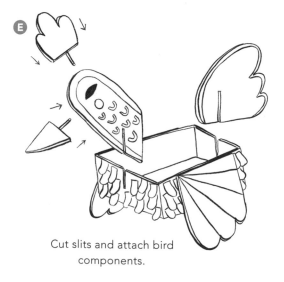

E

Cut slits and attach bird
components.

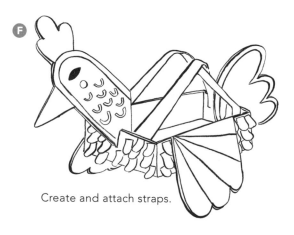

F

Create and attach straps.

8 For the tail feathers, trace the template onto a piece of cardboard. Using scissors or a utility knife, cutting mat, and ruler, cut out the tail shape. Using blue duct tape, cover the exterior edge of the bird tail.

9 For the beak and feather tuft, trace the templates onto pieces of cardboard and cut them out. Cover them each with one color of duct tape, leaving only the edge that will attach to the bird's body uncovered.

10 Push a wooden dowel into the corrugated inside layer of the beak piece and push the opposite end of the dowel into the bird head to attach the beak. Repeat with the second dowel and feather tuft piece (E).

11 Cut a slit in the underside of the head where indicated on the template. Slide the head down over the front of the box (E).

12 Cut a slit in the underside of the tail feather piece where indicated on the template and slide it over the back of the box (E).

13 To create the straps, unroll two 36-inch (90 cm) strips of duct tape. Place one of the strips on top of the other, sticky sides together. Tape one end of the strap to the inside front of the box, and the other end diagonally opposite it on the inside back of the box. Repeat to make the other strap, being sure to cross the straps when attaching the second strap to the box (F).

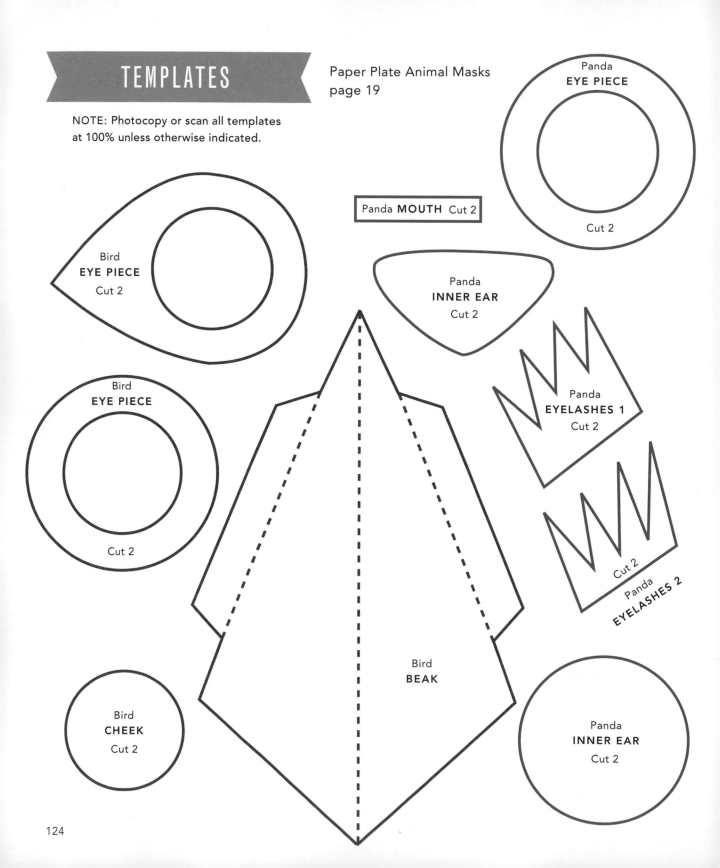

TEMPLATES

Paper Plate Animal Masks
page 19

NOTE: Photocopy or scan all templates at 100% unless otherwise indicated.

Panda **EYE PIECE** Cut 2

Panda **MOUTH** Cut 2

Bird **EYE PIECE** Cut 2

Panda **INNER EAR** Cut 2

Panda **EYELASHES 1** Cut 2

Bird **EYE PIECE** Cut 2

Cut 2
Panda **EYELASHES 2**

Bird **BEAK**

Bird **CHEEK** Cut 2

Panda **INNER EAR** Cut 2

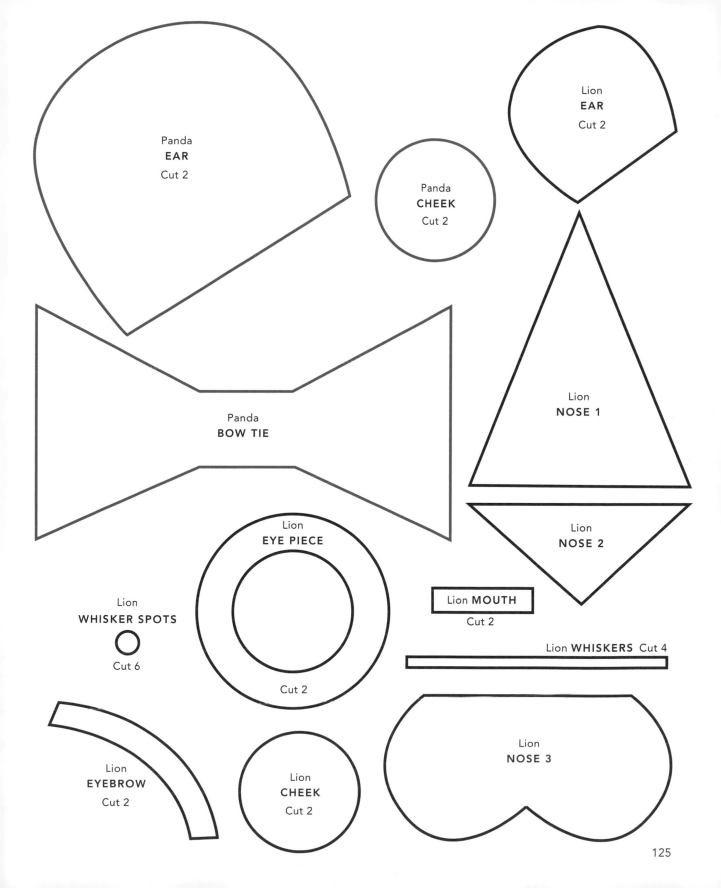

Panda
EAR
Cut 2

Panda
CHEEK
Cut 2

Lion
EAR
Cut 2

Panda
BOW TIE

Lion
NOSE 1

Lion
NOSE 2

Lion
EYE PIECE

Lion **MOUTH**
Cut 2

Lion **WHISKERS** Cut 4

Cut 2

Lion
WHISKER SPOTS

Cut 6

Lion
EYEBROW
Cut 2

Lion
CHEEK
Cut 2

Lion
NOSE 3

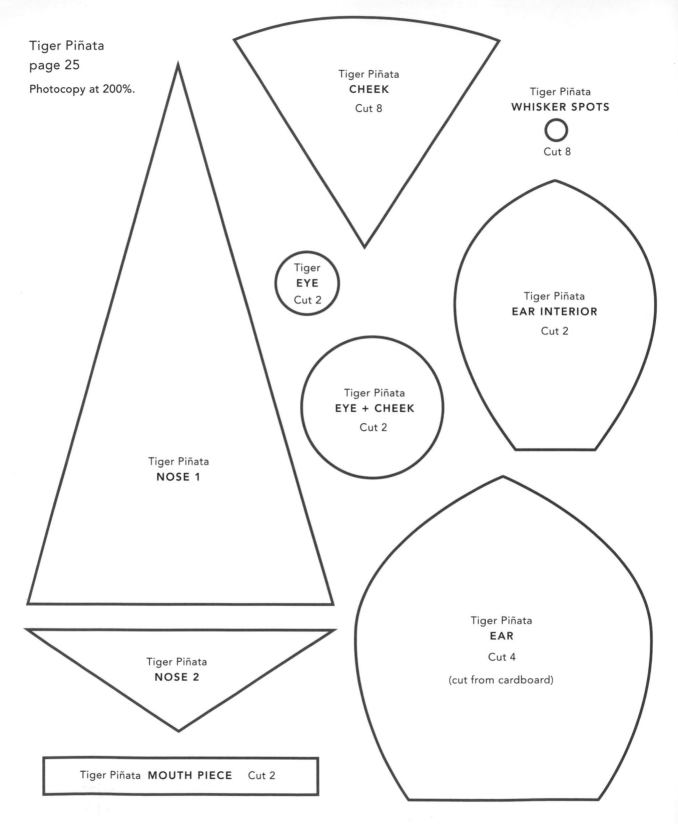

Tiger Piñata
page 25

Photocopy at 200%.

Tiger Piñata
CHEEK

Cut 8

Tiger Piñata
WHISKER SPOTS

Cut 8

Tiger
EYE
Cut 2

Tiger Piñata
EAR INTERIOR

Cut 2

Tiger Piñata
EYE + CHEEK

Cut 2

Tiger Piñata
NOSE 1

Tiger Piñata
NOSE 2

Tiger Piñata
EAR

Cut 4

(cut from cardboard)

Tiger Piñata **MOUTH PIECE**   Cut 2

Knight Smock
page 31

Knight Smock
page 31

Fair Maiden Smock
page 31

Knights and Nobles
Table Tent
page 53

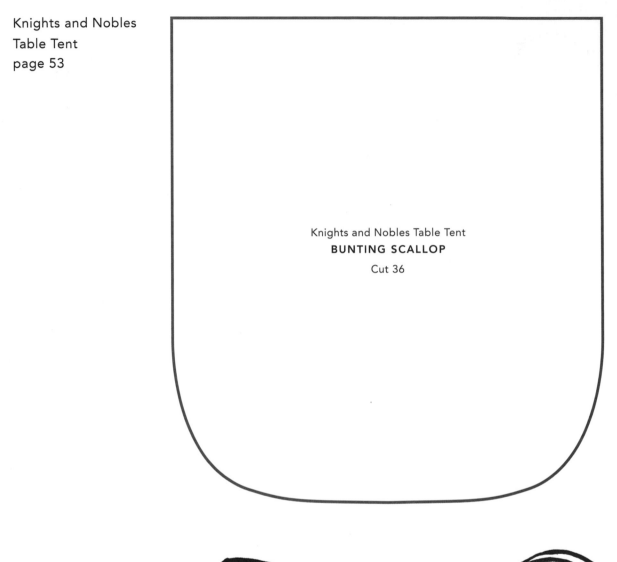

Knights and Nobles Table Tent
BUNTING SCALLOP

Cut 36

Tiered Stacking
Animal Blocks
page 71

Tiered Stacking
Animal Blocks
page 71

Soft Trapeze Doll
page 67
HEAD FRONT

Soft Trapeze Doll
page 67
HEAD BACK

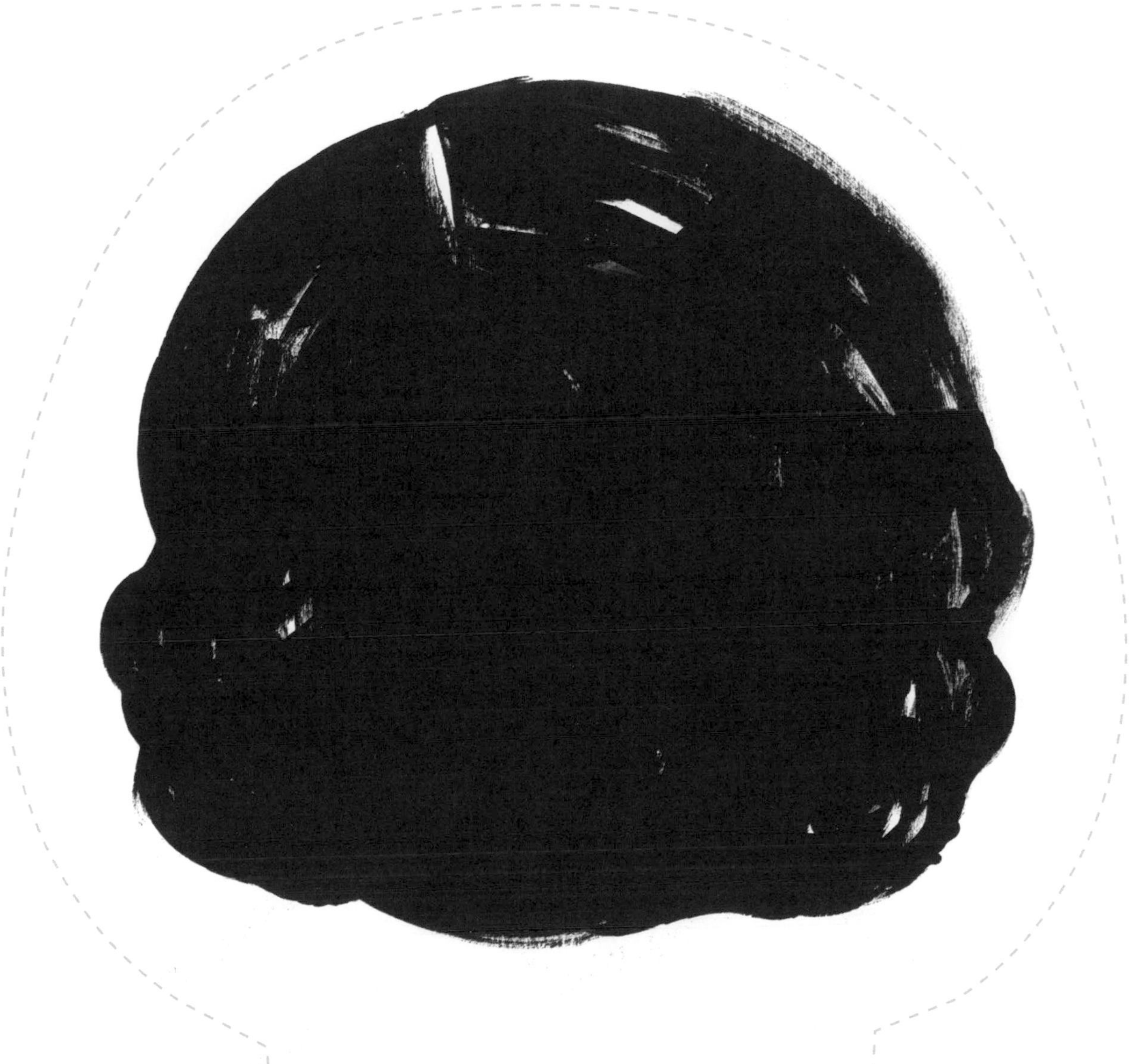

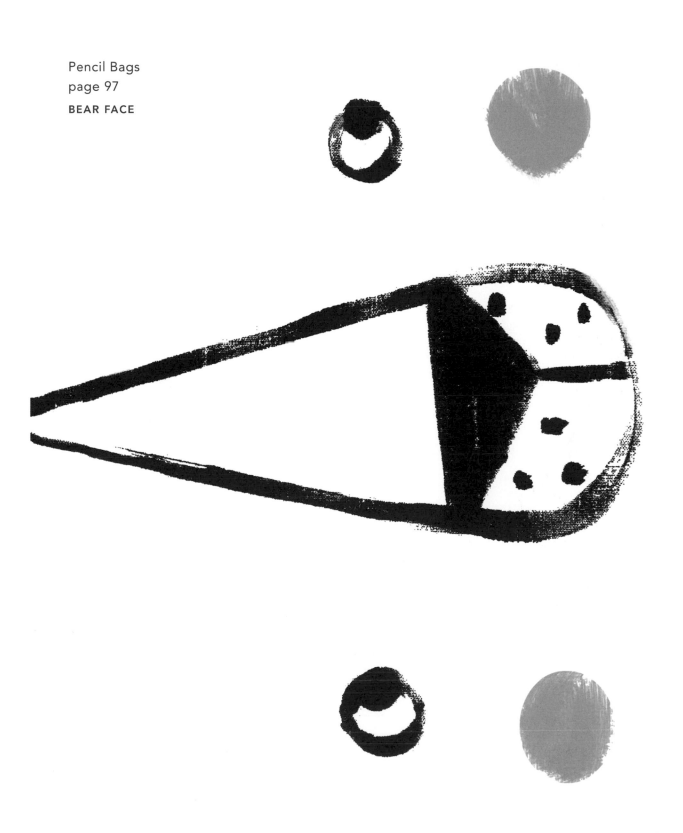

Pencil Bags
page 97
BEAR FACE

SOURCES

I'd love to show you more of what I do, and I'd really like to see the projects you create from this book. Please visit me at my website mermagblog.com.

The materials and tools used to make the projects in this book are generally available at fabric, craft, and home improvement stores. If you cannot find what you are looking for locally, try these resources.

CRAFT AND BUILDING SUPPLIES

www.purlsoho.com (designer and Japanese fabric, wool felt, and yarn)

www.spoonflower.com (one-of-a-kind custom fabric)

www.joann.com (craft wood, regular and printable fabric, stuffing, and supplies)

www.michaels.com (craft wood, regular and printable fabric, stuffing, and supplies)

www.hobbylobby.com (craft wood, regular and printable fabric, stuffing, and supplies)

www.lowes.com (power tools, wood, paint, and supplies)

www.homedepot.com (power tools, wood, paint, and supplies)

www.fedex.com/us/office/ (large format prints)

Following are sources for some of the beautiful clothing and home décor shown in the book.

GENERAL MERCHANDISE

Beware the Moon (for wallpaper)
www.beware-the-moon.com

Colette Bream (for soft toys and home wares)
www.etsy.com/shop/colettebream

Darly Bird (for unique home accessories and gifts) www.darlybird.com

Ez Peduwa (for children's art prints)
www.shopezpudewa.com

Ferm Living (for textiles, pillows, and more)
www.fermlivingshop.com

Flor (for carpet design squares) www.flor.com

Land of Nod (for children's furniture, toys, and home wares) www.landofnod.com

Little Auggie (for children's textiles, bedding, etc.) www.littleauggie.com

Little Baby Company (for children's home décor, party supplies, and more)
www.littlebabycompany.com

Molly-Meg (design shop for children)
www.molly-meg.co.uk

Petit Home (for home accessories and gifts for little ones) www.petithome.co.uk

Pretty Mommy (for unique and handmade
home goods) www.shopprettymommy.com

School House Electric & Supply Co.
(for lighting, furniture, and accessories)
www.schoolhouseelectric.com

The Simpler Life at Perennial Gardens
(for plants)
291 East 140 North
Lindon, Utah 84042
801-318-3431

Sweet Lulu (for party supplies)
www.shopsweetlulu.com

Sycamore Street Press (for wrapping paper
and letterpress prints and cards)
www.sycamorestreetpress.com

Track of Time (for vintage treasures)
www.etsy.com/au/shop/TrackofTime

Treasures Antique Mall (for vintage treasures)
1045 N. 2000 W
Springville, UT 84663
801-491-0749

Zurchers Party Supplies
www.zurchers.com

LOVELY CHILDREN'S CLOTHING

Clotaire
www.chaussuresclotaire.com

GAP Kids
www.gap.com

Goat Milk
www.goatmilknyc.com

Hanna Andersson
www.hannaandersson.com

La Coqueta
www.lacoquetakids.com

Little Vida
www.littlevida.com

Misha Lulu
www.mishalulu.com

Munkstown
www.munkstown.bigcartel.com

Nathalie Verlinden
www.nathalieverlinden.com

Native Shoes
www.nativeshoes.com

Polarn O. Pyret
www.polarnopyretusa.com

PRSPR Kids
www.prsprkids.com

Soor Ploom
www.soorploomclothier.com

Wolf & Rita
www.wolfandrita.com

Wovenplay
www.wovenplay.com

Wunway
www.wunway.com

Zara Kids
www.zara.com

ACKNOWLEDGMENTS

Special thanks to my loving parents, who nurtured an environment steeped in creativity and handmade production. Much love to my dear children for the constant source of inspiration they are to me. Thanks to my incredible husband, Jon, whose never-ending support, encouragement, handyman skills, and many trips to the hardware store literally kept me going. I would also like to thank all of my family, with a special note to Steven, Alisa, Josh, Katie, Annika, Sarah, Ben, and Ava, whose help and support truly made this book possible. And to my friend Brooke Reynolds, who not only designed this book beautifully but who also encouraged me to make it in the first place and introduced me to my editor, Melanie Falick. Of course, a big thanks to Melanie for believing in this project and helping it come to life. To Ivy McFadden and

Cristina Garces for their editing skills. To Nicole Hill Gerulat for her vision behind the camera, making complete magic happen in these beautiful photographs. To Meta Coleman, whose stunning eye for children's design and décor really took this book to the next level and to Brittany Watson Jepsen, whose selection of breathtaking children's clothing delights me every time I look through these pages. To Danielle Wilson for her assistance with sewing and patternmaking. Thanks to the Colemans, the Fords, the Stratfords, and Justin Hackworth for the beautiful photography locations. Of course, a big thank you to all the little ones adorning these pages and to their parents for standing by in the wings. And a huge and heartfelt thank you to all of my mermagblog.com readers and little creative supporters who really make all I do come to life. Thank you. Thank you!

Merrilee